ANCIENT
CIVILIZATIONS

www.dk.com

This book has been specially created by Dorling Kindersley for Family Learning. The Family Learning mission is to support the concept of the home as a center of learning and to help families develop independent learning skills to last a lifetime.

Project editors Gillian Denton, Susan McKeever, Phil Wilkinson
Art editors Martin Atcherley, Liz Sephton
Managing editors Sophie Mitchell, Helen Parker
Managing art editor Julia Harris
Production Louise Barratt, Catherine Semark
Picture research Kathy Lockley, Diana Morris
Additional Photography Lisa Bliss, Kevin Lovelock, John Williams, and Liz McAulay

First American Edition, 1998
2 4 6 8 10 9 7 5 3

Published in the United States by Family Learning
Southland Executive Park
7800 Southland Boulevard, Orlando, Florida 32809

Dorling Kindersley registered offices:
9 Henrietta Street, Covent Garden, London WC2E 8PS

ISBN 0-7894-3789-9

Reproduced in Singapore by Colorscan
Printed in China by Toppan

A Greek drinking cup

A Greek woman wearing a *chiton*

A cast of a Roman snake spirit

EYEWITNESS ⊙ ANTHOLOGIES

ANCIENT CIVILIZATIONS

Written by
Simon James, Anne Pearson,
and Jonathan N. Tubb

A Roman boar
herder

A Roman
cosmetic flask

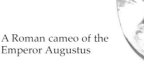

A bronze statue of Heracles, son of Zeus,
a Grecian god

Roman cameos of
the royal family of
Emperor Augustus

A Roman cameo of the
Emperor Augustus

Contents

Introduction

This book shows the great importance of the eastern Mediterranean in creating the major civilizations of the ancient world, from the lands and peoples of the Bible to the Greeks and the Romans. The first part of the book discusses the Canaanites, Israelites, Phoenicians, Assyrians, Babylonians, and Persians, who inhabited the lands from the Dead Sea and the Jordan River to the Sea of Galilee and beyond. The second part examines the world of ancient Greece, from the Minoans and Myceneans to the rise and fall of Sparta, and their literature, drama, philosophy, politics, and sports. The third part analyzes the rising power of Rome and how the terrible might of their soldiers and weaponry helped create the superpower of the Roman Empire.

A pottery mask of the Greek River God

An Assyrian lion-shaped weight

Persian silver goat dating from the 5th century B.C.

A Greek coin showing an owl, the official bird of Athena

A terra-cotta figure of Demeter and Persephone, the Greek goddesses of the grain

A Roman scabbard decorated with gold and silver

Lands of the Bible

THE HOLY LAND is a region of great diversity. From west to east four different kinds of terrain are found. The coastal plain is low-lying and dry in the south, narrowing to the north with stretches of marsh and lagoon. The second zone is the hill country behind the coast, well watered and fertile on the west-facing slopes and rising to rocky ridges that form the spine of the hill country. The third zone, the Jordan Valley, is almost rainless. The highlands of Jordan and the plateau beyond make up the fourth zone. There are rugged mountains in the south of the highlands and rolling hills to the north. The plateau is made up of farmland, giving way to dry steppe country (treeless plains) and finally desert.

Landscape near the Dead Sea

By the Dead Sea, looking east to the hills of Moab

Village of Dir-Zamet, near Hebron

"Lot's wife" – a pillar of rock near the Dead Sea

THE BIBLE LANDS
The Holy Land, also referred to at different times in its history as Palestine and Canaan, lies in the Levant (the eastern Mediterranean). This map shows some of the most important places mentioned in this book, together with the seas and lakes and the River Jordan. North is to the left-hand side of the map.

MOUNT HERMON

Dan

LAKE HULEH

GILEAD

SEA OF GALILEE

JORDAN RIVER

Hazor · Capernaum

Tiberias

Tell es-Sa'idiyeh

Tiwal esh-Sharqi

Beth shan

UPPER GALILEE

LOWER GALILEE

Tirzah

PLAIN OF PHOENICIA

Nazareth

Tyre

Megiddo

Samaria

Acre

Caesarea

MEDITERRANEAN SEA

View of Jerusalem by Carl Werner (1809-1894)

Mount Sinai, south of the map area, was the scene of many of the Old Testament stories

Landscape by the Sea of Galilee

MOAB

EDOM

Qumran

DEAD SEA

Jericho

Masada

Herodium

Jerusalem

Bethlehem

JUDEAN HILLS

Hebron

NEGEV

Lachish

Beer-sheba

Ashdod

PLAIN OF PHILISTIA

Gaza

Modern fishing boats on the Sea of Galilee

CHRONOLOGY OF THE BIBLE LANDS	
Paleolithic (Old Stone Age)	700,000-15,000 B.C.
Mesolithic (Middle Stone Age)	15,000-8,300 B.C.
Neolithic (New Stone Age)	8,300-4,500 B.C.
Chalcolithic	4500-3200 B.C.
Early Bronze Age	3200-2000 B.C.
Middle Bronze Age	2000-1550 B.C.
Late Bronze Age	1550-1150 B.C.
Iron Age	1200-586 B.C.
Babylonian and Persian Periods	586-332 B.C.
Hellenistic Period	332-37 B.C.
Roman Period	37 B.C.-A.D. 324
Byzantine Period	A.D. 324-640
Early Arab Period	A.D. 640-1099

Early ancestors

MUCH OF OUR KNOWLEDGE of the early prehistory of the Holy Land comes from the site of Jericho, near the northern end of the Red Sea. Here, excavations have uncovered a remarkable series of settlements dating back to about 10,000 B.C., when Middle Stone Age (Mesolithic) hunters settled there permanently. At first they built flimsy shelters of sticks and hides, but these were later replaced by houses built of sun-dried mud bricks. In settling down, these people took the all-important step which led in the end to cultivating crops and domesticating (taming and raising) animals – a process known as the "Neolithic revolution." Jericho was not alone. During the following 3,000 years small farming villages sprang up all over the area. During the New Stone Age (or Neolithic, 8300-4500 B.C.) stone, flint, and obsidian (a type of volcanic glass) were used for tools and weapons. The early, pre-pottery phase of the Neolithic is remarkable for its arts and crafts – weaving, basketry, carpentry, and sculpture. Pottery was first made in around 5500 B.C. Knowledge of copper working was acquired about 1,000 years later, during the period known as the Chalcolithic (from the Greek word for copper).

Painted eyes

FACE ART
In the Pre-pottery Neolithic period, people sometimes removed the skull from the skeleton of a dead person. The facial features were re-created in plaster, and hair was painted red or black. Ancestor worship may have been the reason for the sensitive treatment of such skulls. This example was found in Jericho.

FIRST CITY
In the Pre-pottery Neolithic period Jericho grew in a remarkable way. In contrast to the usual simple, unwalled villages, it became a real city, with massive walls and at least one large stone tower, seen here.

SCRAPER
Even after copper working began, flint tools continued to be used. One type is the "fan scraper," which might have been used for preparing animal skins for clothing.

Fan scraper

Scraper

STONY FACE
This finely carved limestone face mask dates to the Pre-pottery Neolithic period. It comes from er-Ram, near Jerusalem, Israel.

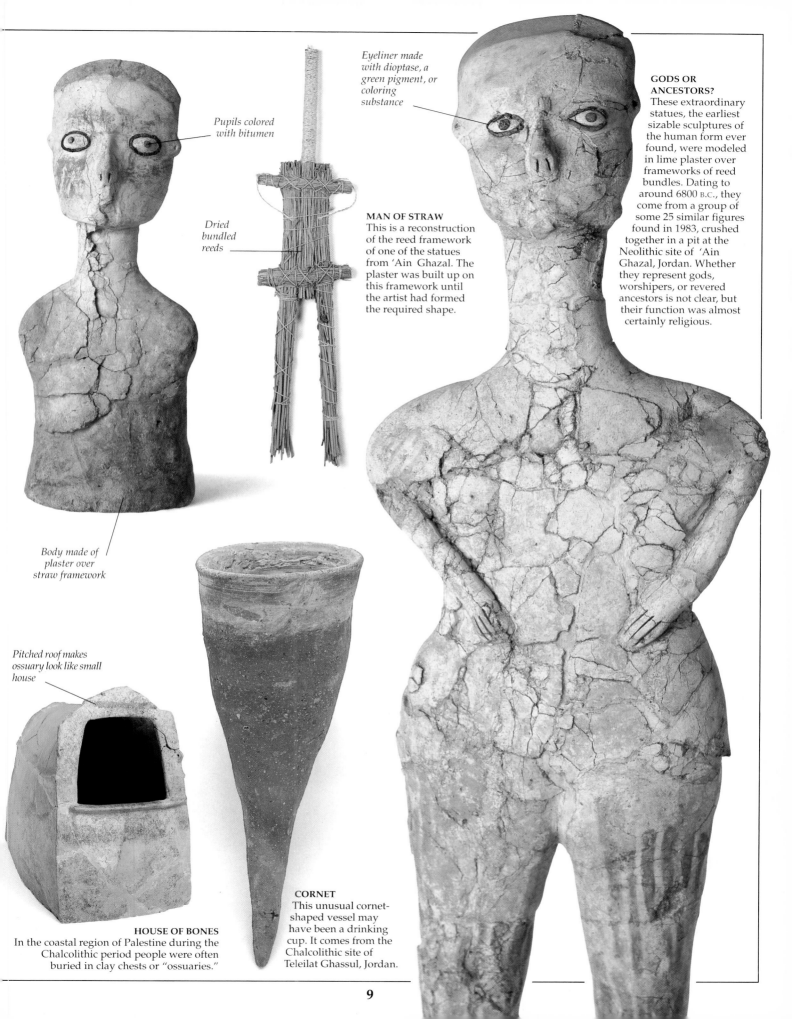

Pupils colored with bitumen

Eyeliner made with dioptase, a green pigment, or coloring substance

Dried bundled reeds

MAN OF STRAW
This is a reconstruction of the reed framework of one of the statues from 'Ain Ghazal. The plaster was built up on this framework until the artist had formed the required shape.

GODS OR ANCESTORS?
These extraordinary statues, the earliest sizable sculptures of the human form ever found, were modeled in lime plaster over frameworks of reed bundles. Dating to around 6800 B.C., they come from a group of some 25 similar figures found in 1983, crushed together in a pit at the Neolithic site of 'Ain Ghazal, Jordan. Whether they represent gods, worshipers, or revered ancestors is not clear, but their function was almost certainly religious.

Body made of plaster over straw framework

Pitched roof makes ossuary look like small house

HOUSE OF BONES
In the coastal region of Palestine during the Chalcolithic period people were often buried in clay chests or "ossuaries."

CORNET
This unusual cornet-shaped vessel may have been a drinking cup. It comes from the Chalcolithic site of Teleilat Ghassul, Jordan.

9

The patriarchs

ABRAHAM, ISAAC, JACOB, AND JOSEPH were the patriarchs of the book of Genesis. They are considered the "founding fathers" of what was to become Israel. Archeology has provided a wealth of information about the time in which their stories are set, and the cultures of the lands through which they are believed to have traveled. The patriarchal stories may have taken place between about 2600 and 1800 B.C., with the tales of Abraham being the earliest, those of Joseph in Egypt the latest. Traditionally, Abraham is said to have gone from Ur in Iraq to the Holy Land, by way of Harran in Turkey. Although there is no archeological proof that this journey took place, there is little doubt that it could have been made.

A gold shell used as a cosmetic container, used in Ur about 4,000 years ago

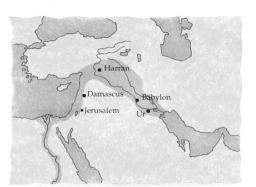

PATRIARCHS' PATH
This map shows the areas between which the patriarchs traveled. They could have gone with trading caravans, or followed the Bedouin, learning the skills of nomadic life.

ROYAL RICHES
At the time of Abraham's departure from Ur, it was a prosperous city. Many of the graves excavated by Sir Leonard Woolley in the 1920s and 1930s were found to contain expensive gifts for the afterlife, such as this ceremonial baton ornamented with gold, lapis lazuli, and mother-of-pearl.

GOLDEN GLORY
An idea of the wealth of the royal family of Ur can be gained from the objects found in their graves, such as this fine gold drinking cup.

TEMPLE TOWER
One of the most important buildings at Ur was the ziggurat, a type of tower built of mud bricks, several stories high, with a temple on top. The biblical Tower of Babel (in the city of Babylon) would have been a similar structure.

Simple bow

Lyre – remains of similar instruments found at Ur

Tunic made of colored and embroidered wool

Bellows, suggesting that some of the people were metalworkers

Duckbill ax (p. 29)

Donkey, one of the earliest beasts of burden

Women wear shoes, in contrast to the men's sandals

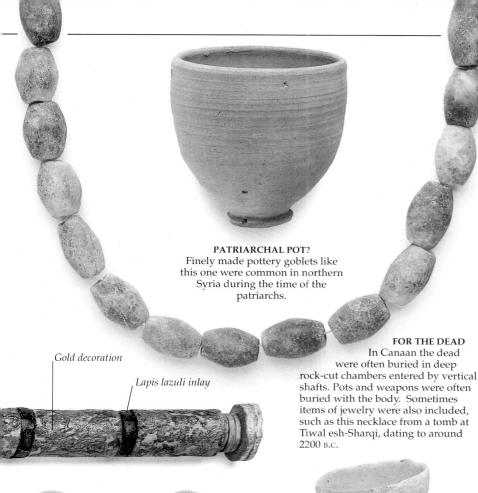

PATRIARCHAL POT?
Finely made pottery goblets like this one were common in northern Syria during the time of the patriarchs.

Gold decoration

Lapis lazuli inlay

FOR THE DEAD
In Canaan the dead were often buried in deep rock-cut chambers entered by vertical shafts. Pots and weapons were often buried with the body. Sometimes items of jewelry were also included, such as this necklace from a tomb at Tiwal esh-Sharqi, dating to around 2200 B.C.

DRINKER'S DELIGHT
This unusual flask from northern Syria was a device for raising liquid. Fluid entered through holes in the base and could be retained by clamping a thumb over the narrow mouth. The liquid could then be released by removing the thumb pressure.

FISHY FLAME
In the patriarchal period the people of Canaan used fish oil in their lamps. It gave such low light that four wicks were needed.

YOGURT MAKER
Yogurt (known as *leben*) has always been an important food in the eastern Mediterranean. This pair of vessels from Jordan is thought to have been used for making yogurt.

Sickle sword

Woolen kilt

Group's leader is called Absha

VISITORS FROM CANAAN
The stories of Joseph's adventures in Egypt are best set in the period 2000-1800 B.C., when archeological evidence has shown that Asiatic people were entering Egypt. These wall paintings are from the tomb of an Egyptian named Amenemhet at Beni Hasan. They show a group of Asiatics, probably Canaanites, being introduced to the Egyptian court.

Egypt

IN THE EARLY BRONZE AGE the opening of trade routes to Egypt allowed a thriving city-based economy to develop in Canaan. In the Middle Bronze Age, groups of Canaanites moved into northern Egypt and established a local dynasty called the Hyksos, who eventually took over the whole of Egypt. Only in the Late Bronze Age, in about 1550 B.C., did the Egyptian pharaohs expel the Hyksos, launch a military campaign against Canaan, and bring it under Egyptian control. Egypt imposed heavy taxes on Canaan, but in return the Canaanite cities gained security and better access to international markets. In the reign of Ramses II (1304-1237 B.C.), the empire was reorganized. Key strategic cities like Beth Shan and Gaza were strengthened, others were allowed to decline. Many people were made homeless and migrated to the Judean hill country, where they established small farming settlements. These dispossessed Canaanites, known to the Egyptians as Hapiru (or Hebrews), formed the basis of what was to become Israel.

EGYPT AND CANAAN
In the Late Bronze Age Canaan became part of the Egyptian Empire. Her local rulers became vassals of the pharaoh. Some of the cities of Canaan, like Gaza, prospered under the Egyptians.

LOST AND FOUND
According to the Bible, Moses, leader of the Hebrew exodus (departure from Egypt), was found in the bulrushes.

POWER SYMBOL
This Egyptian ceremonial ax has an elaborate openwork head.

LETTER TO THE PHARAOH
The Armana letters contain reports from vassal rulers of the empire to Egyptian pharaoh Amenophis III. Some mention trouble caused by lawless bands of "Hapiru," homeless peoples living on the fringes of cities. The Hapiru are related to the biblical Hebrews.

STRONGHOLD
Beth Shan was one of the major centers of Egyptian control in Canaan. During the time of Ramses II, the city was occupied by Egyptian troops and had an Egyptian governor.

HEBREW SLAVES?
Both the Bible and an Egyptian papyrus refer to "Hapiru" employed as laborers in Ramses II's building projects. They may not actually have been slaves, as suggested in this detail of a painting by 19th-century artist Sir Edward Poynter.

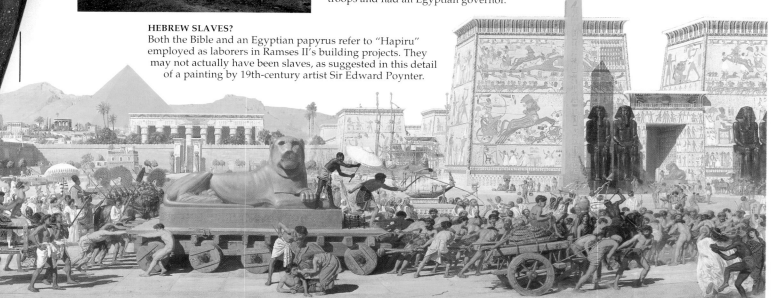

PHILISTINE FACE
The Philistines, like some of the other sea peoples, buried their dead in distinctive "slipper-shaped" coffins. The lids show grotesquely modeled human features.

The Philistines

In Ramses III's reign (1198-1166 B.C.), the Egyptian Empire faced a major crisis when it was invaded by a league of peoples from the Aegean (the Greek islands) and southern Anatolia (modern Turkey). Known as the sea peoples, they included a group called the Philistines. Ramses pushed them back from the shores of Egypt in a great naval battle. But he could not stop them from settling in Canaan, at the southern end of the coastal strip.

FINE FEATHERS
Philistine warriors wore feathered headdresses.

SUCCESSFUL PHARAOH
Ramses II brought to an end Egypt's long conflict with the Hittites of Anatolia. After fighting the Hittites at the Battle of Kadesh in 1289 B.C., the Egyptians signed a treaty which brought them a period of peace and prosperity. Ramses II was most probably the pharaoh of the biblical exodus.

Striped headcloth indicates kingship

After Ramses II reorganized his empire the number of hill-farming settlements in Judea increased dramatically.

PARTING OF THE WATERS
Although archeology cannot confirm the story of the Hebrew exodus through the waters of the Red Sea, it is not unlikely that a group of "Hapiru" left Egypt during the reign of Ramses II and found their way to the Judean hill country.

The Canaanites

STAR ATTRACTION
This finely made star pendant from Tell el-'Ajjul shows the skill of the Canaanite goldsmiths of the 16th century B.C.

THE FULL FLOWERING of Canaanite culture came in the Middle Bronze Age (c. 2000-1550 B.C.). During this period Canaan was largely free of the power struggles and foreign interventions that were to dominate its later history. In this climate, the country developed an ever-expanding trade network. There was extensive trade with Egypt, and contacts were strengthened with Syria, Anatolia, and Cyprus. Canaan's art, architecture, and craftsmanship reached new levels of skill and sophistication as her artists were influenced by a variety of sources and countries. During the Late Bronze Age (1550-1150 B.C.) Canaan was dominated by Egypt. The Egyptian empire brought with it even more far-reaching trade links, including those with the Mycenaean people of mainland Greece. But the local culture, by now well established, continued to flourish.

THE LAND OF CANAAN
We do not know exactly how Palestine was structured politically during the Middle Bronze Age. It was probably made up of a large number of independent city states, each ruled by a prince. Each city would have controlled its own area of land containing a number of dependent towns and villages.

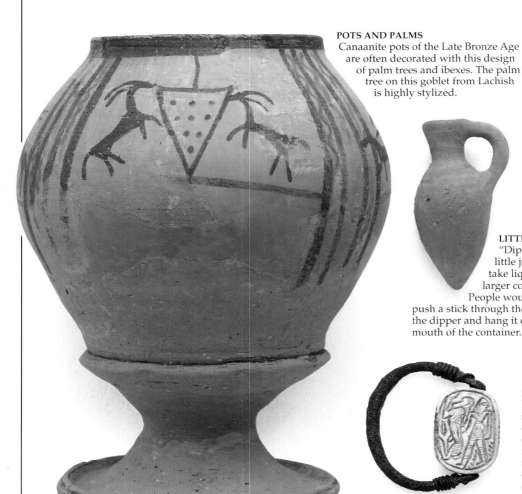

POTS AND PALMS
Canaanite pots of the Late Bronze Age are often decorated with this design of palm trees and ibexes. The palm tree on this goblet from Lachish is highly stylized.

LITTLE DIPPER
"Dippers" were little jugs used to take liquid out of a larger container. People would often push a stick through the handle of the dipper and hang it over the mouth of the container.

PILGRIM'S PLEASURE
The Canaanites were very inventive. This amusing pilgrim flask, dating to the end of the Late Bronze Age, has its own built-in drinking cup.

SEAL OF APPROVAL
Egyptian-style seals and scarabs (seals in the shape of a beetle), used to denote ownership, were common in Canaan. Many were made by Canaanite craftsmen, and some were exported to Egypt.

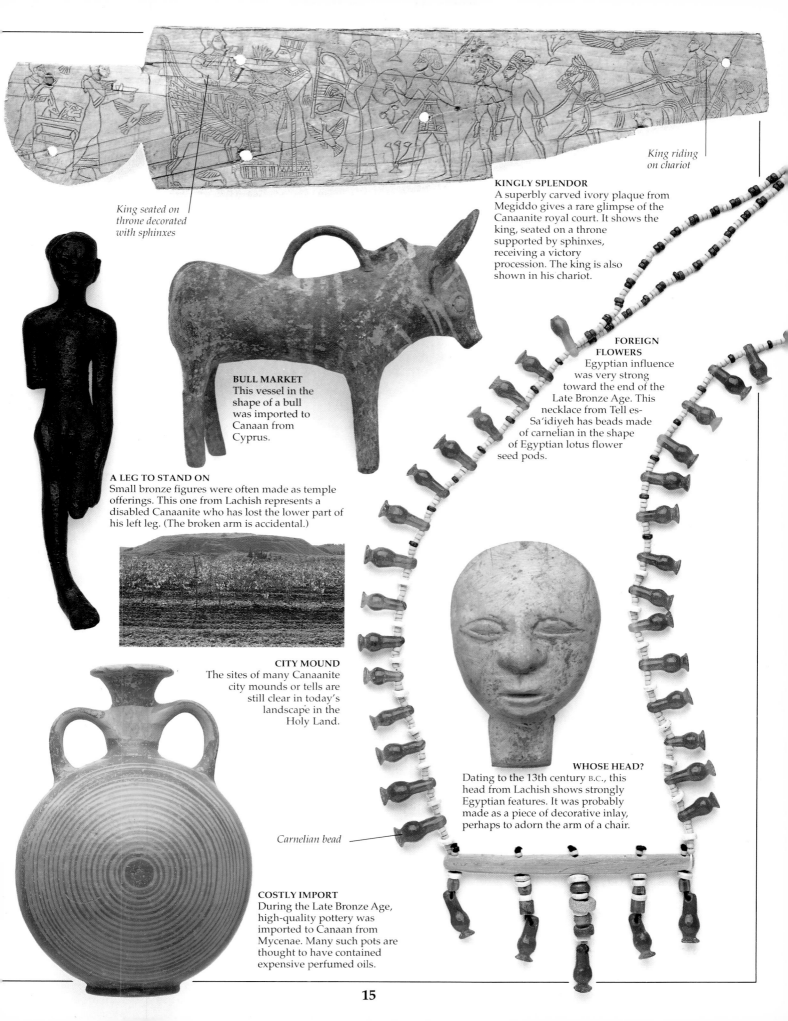

King seated on throne decorated with sphinxes

King riding on chariot

KINGLY SPLENDOR
A superbly carved ivory plaque from Megiddo gives a rare glimpse of the Canaanite royal court. It shows the king, seated on a throne supported by sphinxes, receiving a victory procession. The king is also shown in his chariot.

BULL MARKET
This vessel in the shape of a bull was imported to Canaan from Cyprus.

FOREIGN FLOWERS
Egyptian influence was very strong toward the end of the Late Bronze Age. This necklace from Tell es-Sa'idiyeh has beads made of carnelian in the shape of Egyptian lotus flower seed pods.

A LEG TO STAND ON
Small bronze figures were often made as temple offerings. This one from Lachish represents a disabled Canaanite who has lost the lower part of his left leg. (The broken arm is accidental.)

CITY MOUND
The sites of many Canaanite city mounds or tells are still clear in today's landscape in the Holy Land.

Carnelian bead

WHOSE HEAD?
Dating to the 13th century B.C., this head from Lachish shows strongly Egyptian features. It was probably made as a piece of decorative inlay, perhaps to adorn the arm of a chair.

COSTLY IMPORT
During the Late Bronze Age, high-quality pottery was imported to Canaan from Mycenae. Many such pots are thought to have contained expensive perfumed oils.

Delicate ivory furniture ornament from Samaria

The Israelites

By ABOUT 1150 B.C., the Egyptians had effectively withdrawn from Canaan, leaving a vacuum to be filled by the Israelites and the Philistines. For nearly 100 years they lived side by side, the Philistines on the coastal plain, the Israelites in the more barren hill country. But during the 11th century B.C., the Philistines tried to extend their territory. Faced with this threat, the Israelites united into one nation under the leadership of first Saul, then David. In about 1000 B.C. David captured Jerusalem and was proclaimed king of the Israelite nation. He finally defeated the Philistines and expanded Israel's territory. The kingdom continued to flourish under David's son Solomon, who extended Israel's trading network and built the Great Temple in Jerusalem. After Solomon's death in 928 B.C., tensions between the north and south of the kingdom came to a head. The monarchy finally split in two. The capital of Judah, in the south, was Jerusalem; Israel, in the north, had its capital at Samaria.

NO SMOKE WITHOUT FIRE
This lively 19th-century engraving represents the destruction of the Temple by the Babylonians in 587 B.C.

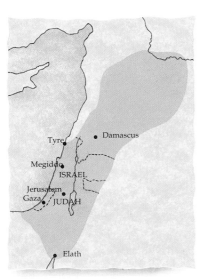

THE TWO KINGDOMS
This map shows the area of David's kingdom, which divided into two: Israel in the north and Judah in the south.

FIRST MENTION OF ISRAEL
This stela (stone marker) of the pharaoh Merneptah (1235-1223 B.C.) records a military campaign in Canaan directed against Gezer, Ashkelon, and Israel. This is the first recorded mention of Israel as a political unit, representing the farming communities of the Judean hill country.

BOTTOMS UP
Probably a furniture ornament, this ivory fragment from King Ahab's palace at Samaria shows the hindquarters of a lion. Relations between Israel and Phoenicia (pp. 18-19) were close, and Phoenician artisans were often used for fine work such as this.

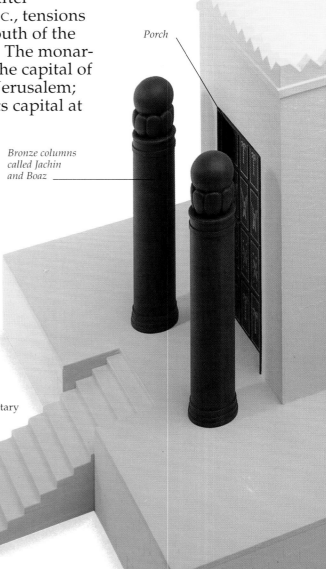

Porch

Bronze columns called Jachin and Boaz

16

Solomon's Temple

Wealth from trade, and a good central administration, enabled Solomon to carry out large-scale building projects. Impressive public buildings, gateways, and city walls were built at several major sites. The most important project was the Temple in Jerusalem. No traces of the building can be seen now, but there are detailed descriptions of it in the Bible. This evidence, together with excavations at other sites, has made possible various reconstructions of the Temple like the one shown here.

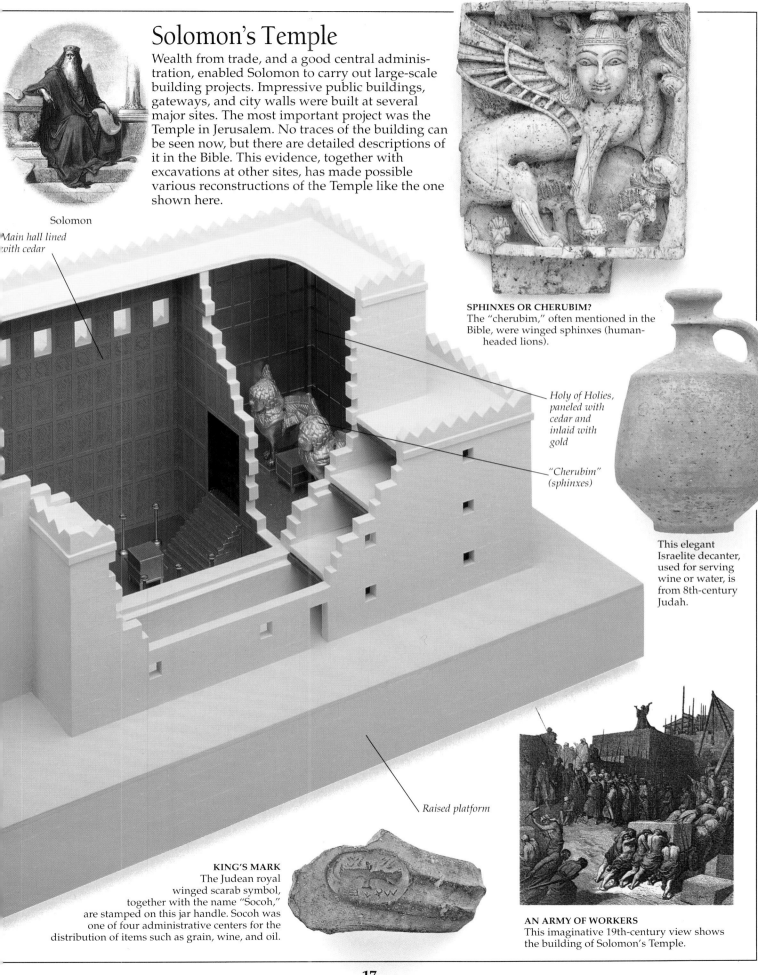

Solomon

Main hall lined with cedar

SPHINXES OR CHERUBIM?
The "cherubim," often mentioned in the Bible, were winged sphinxes (human-headed lions).

Holy of Holies, paneled with cedar and inlaid with gold

"Cherubim" (sphinxes)

This elegant Israelite decanter, used for serving wine or water, is from 8th-century Judah.

Raised platform

KING'S MARK
The Judean royal winged scarab symbol, together with the name "Socoh," are stamped on this jar handle. Socoh was one of four administrative centers for the distribution of items such as grain, wine, and oil.

AN ARMY OF WORKERS
This imaginative 19th-century view shows the building of Solomon's Temple.

The Phoenicians

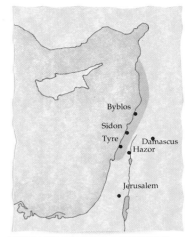

BY THE SECOND MILLENIUM B.C. the Israelites occupied most of Palestine except for the southern coastal strip, which was held by the Philistines. To the north, the powerful Aramean kingdoms controlled most of central and northern Syria. The remaining Canaanite territory, in the northwest, became Phoenicia. The name derives from the Greek word for "purple," because the Phoenician cities were well known for their technique of purple fabric dyeing (p. 27). There was little farming land in Phoenicia, so the people turned to the sea to make a living, becoming great seafarers and traders. The Phoenicians were also excellent craft workers, and their work was in demand all over the Middle East. Solomon is said to have employed Phoenician workers to build his temple in Jerusalem.

The Phoenician writing on this seal identifies its owner as "Tamak-el, son of Milkam"

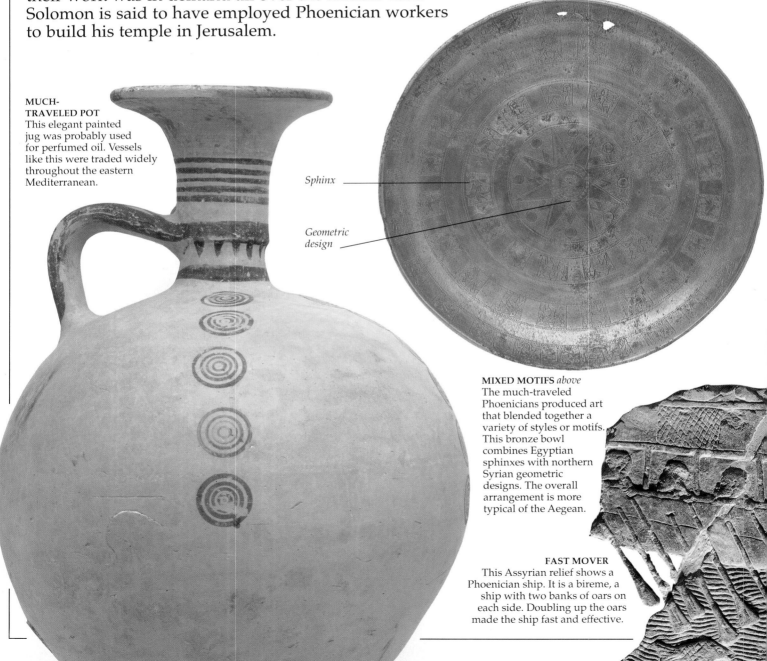

MUCH-TRAVELED POT
This elegant painted jug was probably used for perfumed oil. Vessels like this were traded widely throughout the eastern Mediterranean.

Sphinx

Geometric design

MIXED MOTIFS *above*
The much-traveled Phoenicians produced art that blended together a variety of styles or motifs. This bronze bowl combines Egyptian sphinxes with northern Syrian geometric designs. The overall arrangement is more typical of the Aegean.

FAST MOVER
This Assyrian relief shows a Phoenician ship. It is a bireme, a ship with two banks of oars on each side. Doubling up the oars made the ship fast and effective.

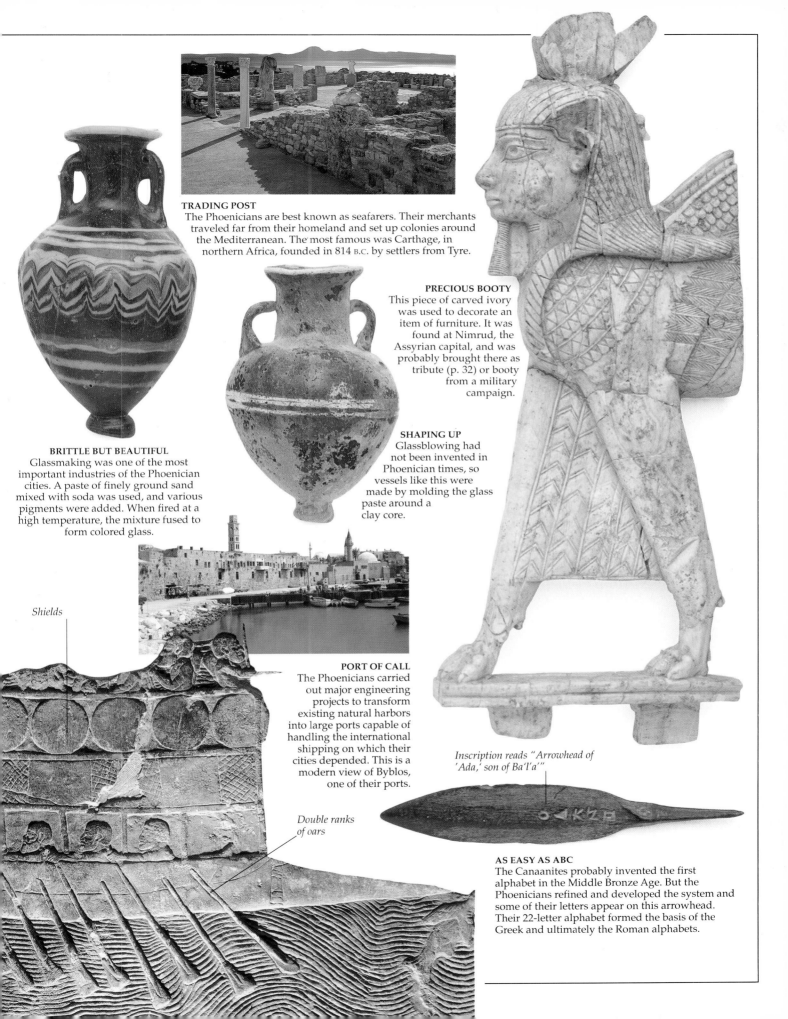

TRADING POST
The Phoenicians are best known as seafarers. Their merchants traveled far from their homeland and set up colonies around the Mediterranean. The most famous was Carthage, in northern Africa, founded in 814 B.C. by settlers from Tyre.

PRECIOUS BOOTY
This piece of carved ivory was used to decorate an item of furniture. It was found at Nimrud, the Assyrian capital, and was probably brought there as tribute (p. 32) or booty from a military campaign.

BRITTLE BUT BEAUTIFUL
Glassmaking was one of the most important industries of the Phoenician cities. A paste of finely ground sand mixed with soda was used, and various pigments were added. When fired at a high temperature, the mixture fused to form colored glass.

SHAPING UP
Glassblowing had not been invented in Phoenician times, so vessels like this were made by molding the glass paste around a clay core.

Shields

PORT OF CALL
The Phoenicians carried out major engineering projects to transform existing natural harbors into large ports capable of handling the international shipping on which their cities depended. This is a modern view of Byblos, one of their ports.

Double ranks of oars

Inscription reads "Arrowhead of 'Ada,' son of Ba'l'a'"

AS EASY AS ABC
The Canaanites probably invented the first alphabet in the Middle Bronze Age. But the Phoenicians refined and developed the system and some of their letters appear on this arrowhead. Their 22-letter alphabet formed the basis of the Greek and ultimately the Roman alphabets.

Worship

UNTIL THE ISRAELITE concept of the "One God" was widely accepted, religion in the Holy Land involved the worship of a variety of gods and goddesses. These gods were thought to dominate every aspect of life – war, weather, fertility, the harvest, and so on. Most of what we know about them comes from a large archive of clay tablets, dating to the Late Bronze Age, found at the site of Ras Shamra, Syria. The tablets tell of the supreme god, El, the "father of man," whose domain was the heavens. His wife, Asherah, ruled over the seas. Their children made up a group of over 70 other deities (gods) including the storm and warrior god, Baal, and the goddess of love and fertility, Astarte.

FERTILITY FIGURE
Astarte, the Canaanite goddess of fertility, is depicted on this gold plaque. It comes from a hoard of goldwork found at Tell el-'Ajjul, dating to the 16th century B.C.

EARLY GOD?
The lime-plaster statues from 'Ain Ghazal (p. 9) probably served some ritual function, but whether they were meant to represent gods or their worshipers is unknown.

WARRIOR GOD
This bronze figure, ornamented with silver, dates to the Late Bronze Age. It is thought to represent the god Baal, who is depicted as a warrior, brandishing his weapon.

POPULAR DEITY
Perhaps the most powerful and popular Canaanite goddess, Astarte is usually shown naked, with her hands cupping her breasts. This plaque of Astarte is made of terra-cotta.

BAAL'S PROPHETS
King Ahab married Jezebel, a Phoenician princess who reestablished worship of the god Baal in Israel. The prophet Elijah called upon God to light a sacrificial fire in front of the prophets of Baal, to show His superiority.

BY THE LIGHT OF THE MOON
This Canaanite temple, excavated at Hazor, was dedicated to the worship of the moon god and his wife.

EGYPTIAN EYE
The eye of Horus was one of the most popular Egyptian amulets (charms). Representing the god Horus in both human and falcon form, it combines a human eye with a falcon's feather.

WHOSE HAND?
Although many Canaanite temples and shrines have been excavated throughout Palestine, we do not usually know which gods and goddesses were worshiped in them. This finely carved ivory hand was all that remained of a statue from the "fosse" temple at Lachish.

GOD OF WINE
This bust of the Nabatean (Arab) vine god Dushara is from the temple of Dushara at Si'a in the Hauran, southern Syria. It is carved in black basalt, a very hard local stone.

The facade of the Temple at Jerusalem depicted on a coin of Simon Bar Kochba, leader of the second Jewish revolt (p. 25)

ASTARTE LIVES ON
Despite Israelite religious laws prohibiting the worship of other gods and goddesses, models of Canaanite fertility goddesses, such as Astarte, continued to be produced throughout the Iron Age.

GODS OF EGYPT *left*
The gods of conquering powers were often worshiped alongside the Canaanite gods. Egyptian amulets appeared in the Late Bronze Age, when Canaan was ruled by Egypt; they remained popular in the Iron Age. These 9th-century B.C. amulets show the sphinx, with a cat's body and a woman's head, and Sekhmet, goddess of the burning heat of the sun.

Sekhmet   Sekhmet   Sphinx   Sekhmet

GODS OF GREECE
The Greek domination of Syria and Palestine after 332 B.C. brought with it the Greek religion and its gods and goddesses. Many of these became equated with traditional deities – for example, the Greek goddess Aphrodite took on the role of Astarte.

Arts and crafts

Some of the earliest people of the Holy Land were skilled in the arts and crafts, producing items of beauty for religious purposes and as status symbols. Those who made the lime-plaster statues found at 'Ain Ghazal (pp. 8-9) in the Stone Age had great expertise. They also displayed great refinement in the way they applied the decoration to the statues. Wonderfully carved ivories and elaborate copper objects are found in the following Chalcolithic period. But it was the Canaanites of the Bronze Age and the Phoenicians of the Iron Age who turned this tradition of skillful work into a real industry, producing arts and crafts that were much admired and sought after throughout the eastern Mediterranean and beyond.

FOR SHOW
In the Middle Bronze Age, metal-casting techniques became more and more sophisticated. This bronze axhead, decorated with a lion fighting a dog, was probably for ceremonial use.

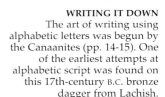

Incised alphabetic writing

DAILY LIFE IN ANCIENT JERICHO
Wooden furniture was preserved in some of the tombs in Jericho. Canaanite carpenters had an extensive tool kit. They put their products together using accurate joints and deco-rated them with carving.

MUSIC MAKERS
Dancing and music were undoubtedly popular activities throughout the history of Palestine, although few instruments have survived. Written descriptions and pictures suggest the use of a wide variety of instruments, such as harps, lyres, flutes, trumpets, and a range of percussion instruments.

WRITING IT DOWN
The art of writing using alphabetic letters was begun by the Canaanites (pp. 14-15). One of the earliest attempts at alphabetic script was found on this 17th-century B.C. bronze dagger from Lachish.

IVORY QUEENS
The Canaanites and Phoenicians were renowned for their ivory carving. Ivory was often used for inlays and furniture ornaments. Some ivory objects have letters on the back to show where they should be attached. This example is a 9th-century Phoenician ivory from the Assyrian city of Nimrud. It shows two seated queens in Egyptian style and was decorated with blue glass and gold overlay.

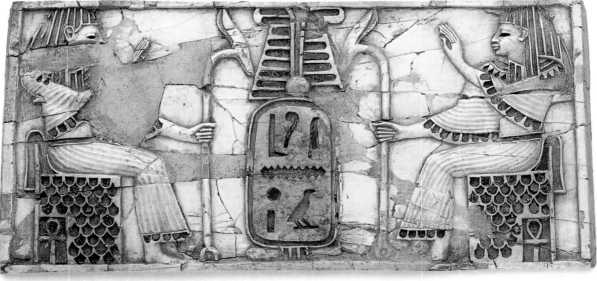

HARD TO CARVE

The combat between a lion and a dog seems to have been a popular subject for the Canaanites. This example is carved on a piece of black basalt, a very hard stone which took great skill to work. It dates to the 14th century B.C. and comes from Beth Shan.

Applied gold decoration

Most of the methods of the ancient potter are still used today. Here a village potter in Egypt produces simple domestic wares.

SYRIAN STYLE

This ivory female head was found at Nimrud. Its style of carving lacks the sophistication of the Phoenician piece opposite. It might have been the work of a Syrian carver.

FUNNY FACE

The finest pottery ever seen in Palestine, in terms of both technical quality and beauty, was made by the Canaanites. Their potters also had a sense of humor, as shown by this extraordinary face vase from Jericho, dating to the 6th century B.C.

GOLDEN GRAINS

This fine pendant comes from Tell el-'Ajjul and dates to the 16th century B.C. It is decorated by granulation. In this process gold wire is melted to make tiny beads, which are then soldered to the surface.

Granulation

CARVED IN STONE

Vessels carved from stone such as calcite and alabaster were extremely popular in the Late Bronze and Iron Ages, perhaps as containers for perfumed oil. This example comes from Tell es-Sa'idiyeh.

TREASURES OF THE TEMPLE

When the Egyptians left Canaan they took the best artists and craftworkers. So Solomon asked the king of Tyre for Phoenician artisans when building his temple in Jerusalem. Phoenician metalworkers probably made the temple furnishings mentioned in the Bible and shown in this old engraving.

Money and trade

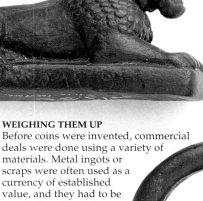

THE HOLY LAND is at the heart of the Fertile Crescent. This made it a corridor for international traders. Merchants traveled between Egypt and Arabia in the south, Anatolia and Mesopotamia in the north; there was also maritime (sea) trade with the Mediterranean islands. These contacts go back a long way. In the New Stone Age period there was trade in obsidian, a black volcanic glass that was used to make tools. But it was the growth of cities in the third millennium B.C. that really laid the foundations for the trade that would sustain the civilizations of the area for thousands of years. In Palestine, farming developed so that surpluses of cereals, flour, oil, and wine could be exported to foreign markets. Canaanite arts and craft objects were also exported widely. Raw materials such as wood and metal came in from abroad.

Found at Amathus in Cyprus, this Phoenician glass vessel was probably used to hold incense

WEIGHING THEM UP
Before coins were invented, commercial deals were done using a variety of materials. Metal ingots or scraps were often used as a currency of established value, and they had to be weighed so that their worth could be assessed. So accurate weights were needed, like these lion-shaped ones from Assyria. They are inscribed with the name of King Shalmaneser III, for whom they were made.

During their first revolt against Rome in A.D. 66 (p. 45), the Jews struck their own coins

WAGON TRAIN
A pottery model of a covered wagon from Hamman in Syria shows the type of vehicle that was used to transport goods in the late 3rd millennium B.C. Wagons like this might have been used by traveling metalworkers, peddling their wares from town to town.

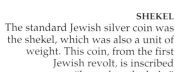

SHEKEL
The standard Jewish silver coin was the shekel, which was also a unit of weight. This coin, from the first Jewish revolt, is inscribed "Jerusalem the holy."

STOPPING ON THE WAY
This detail of an evocative painting by Edward Lear (1812-1888) shows a desert caravan stopping by Mount Sinai. It gives a good idea of what long-distance caravan traffic must have been like in ancient times.

ROMAN CASH
Coins came into common use in the Holy Land at the time of the conquest of Alexander (p. 44). Roman imperial coins bore a portrait of the emperor, in this case, Vespasian.

ONE HUMP OR TWO?
Two-humped Bactrian camels appear on the Assyrian Black Obelisk. These creatures did not appear in the Holy Land until Solomon's time. Before that, trading caravans relied on the one-humped Arabian camel.

A coin of the second Jewish revolt (A.D. 132-135) bears the name of its leader, Simon Bar Kochba

MAN OF THE PEOPLE?
These bronze coins are from the reign of Herod's son Archelaus (4 B.C.–A.D. 6). One shows a crested helmet, the other a bunch of grapes. The Greek inscription reads "Herod, governor of the people."

Because coins circulated widely, they could be used to promote a cause or idea. These two from the second Jewish revolt bear inscriptions. The first reads "Year one of the redemption of Israel"; the second bears the name of the leader Simon Bar Kochba.

POPPY POWER
During the Late Bronze Age little jugs known as "bil-bils" were imported into Canaan. Analysis of substances found inside some of them has shown that they were used to hold the drug opium. The shape of the jug is strikingly like that of an upturned poppy head.

25

Continued on next page

A bronze coin of Agrippa I (A.D. 37-44), grandson of Herod the Great. He used the umbrella as a symbol of monarchy.

INSTEAD OF MONEY
Precious metals were frequently traded as ingots. This silver ingot is from Zinjirli, ancient Sam'al.

TURNING THE TABLES
Jesus of Nazareth objected to merchants trading their wares in the precincts of the Temple in Jerusalem and toppled the stalls and tables.

COMMEMORATION
Coins could be made to commemorate famous events. This coin, inscribed "Judaea Capta," records the Roman victory in the first Jewish revolt (p. 45).

Handles of this shape give this vessel the name "stirrup jar"

IMPORT
Beautifully made and elegantly decorated, Mycenaean vessels known as "stirrup jars" were imported into Canaan during the Late Bronze Age, perhaps containing perfumed oils.

STORAGE JAR
In the 12th century B.C., Tell es-Sa'idiyeh, on the eastern side of the Jordan River, was an Egyptian taxation and distribution center, collecting produce from Jordan for shipment to Egypt. Jars of Egyptian design were found in one of the storerooms at the site and may have been used to store and transport wine.

MERCHANT SHIP OF SOLOMON'S FLEET
King Solomon was intent upon developing a wide network of sea trade relations. With the co-operation of Hiram, king of Tyre, he built a major port at Ezion Geber at the head of the Red Sea. A joint Israelite and Phoenician fleet was based there, and every three years, ships set sail for "Ophir" (probably the Somali coast of East Africa) in search of fine gold.

SEA HORSES
Timber was always a valuable item of trade. The most expensive and sought-after wood came from the "Cedars of Lebanon." This 8th-century B.C. Assyrian relief shows Phoenician merchant ships hauling logs along the Syrian coast. These ships were called hippoi, meaning horses, as they had horse figureheads.

8 shekels

"Neseph," five sixths of a shekel

"Beqa," half a shekel

HOW HEAVY?
The ancient Palestinian system of weights was based on the shekel (equivalent to about 0.4 oz [11.4 g]), the mina (60 shekels) and the kikkar or "talent" (60 minas). These stone weights are inscribed in Hebrew with their value.

LONG-DISTANCE TRADER *above*
This Roman merchant ship, known as a corbita, has two masts. Its sails are made of oblong blocks of cloth sewn together and reinforced with leather patches at the corners. Such vessels were used for long-distance shipping across the Mediterranean rather than for coastal use.

LIGHTING THE WAY
Pharos, the lighthouse of Alexandria, the port city and capital of Egypt founded by Alexander the Great, was one of the seven wonders of the ancient world.

ROYAL PURPLE
One of the most sought-after items traded by Phoenician merchants was their purple-dyed cloth. By the time of the Roman Empire, its prestige was so great that it could only be worn by the emperor.

THEIR TRUE COLORS
The highly prized purple dye for which the Phoenicians are renowned was extracted from a gland of the murex snail. Each snail yielded only a drop of yellow liquid which darkened on exposure to light. Processing required slow simmering for about two weeks. Up to 60,000 snails were needed for each pound of dye. Different tints were achieved by varying the amount of extract from different species.

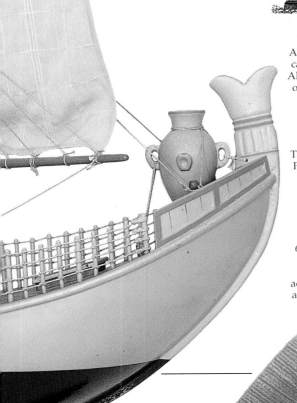

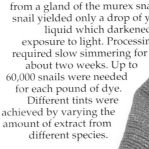

Weaponry

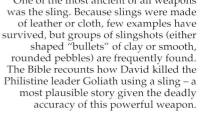

This relief shows an Aramean cavalryman of the 9th century B.C. It comes from Tell Halaf, the biblical Gozan.

FROM THE EARLIEST TIMES weapons were used for hunting and to protect people against their enemies. Until copper smelting was invented sometime before 4000 B.C., the people of the Holy Land made weapons out of wood, bone, and stone. As the Early Bronze Age cities grew, the techniques of warfare developed and armies were established. The more advanced metalworking of this period provided soldiers with mass-produced swords, spears, and axes. Initially these were made of copper, later of bronze. Later in the Bronze Age war and weapons became more sophisticated, with field battles involving cavalry and chariots; well-defended cities were attacked using special siege equipment. The Philistines probably brought ironworking to Canaan around 1200 B.C; after this, iron weapons gradually replaced bronze ones.

GIANT-SLAYER
One of the most ancient of all weapons was the sling. Because slings were made of leather or cloth, few examples have survived, but groups of slingshots (either shaped "bullets" of clay or smooth, rounded pebbles) are frequently found. The Bible recounts how David killed the Philistine leader Goliath using a sling – a most plausible story given the deadly accuracy of this powerful weapon.

Pair of helmets from the Persian period

TAKING AIM
This slinger is depicted on a 9th-century B.C. relief from the royal palace at Tell Halaf (Gozan), Syria.

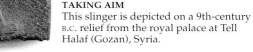

GOOD GRIP
The hilt of this Late Bronze Age dagger from Alalakh in Syria was cast with deep recesses to allow a wooden or bone grip to be inserted.

Broad cutting blade

Sword would have been attached to wooden or bone hilt with copper rivets

Ridge to make blade stronger

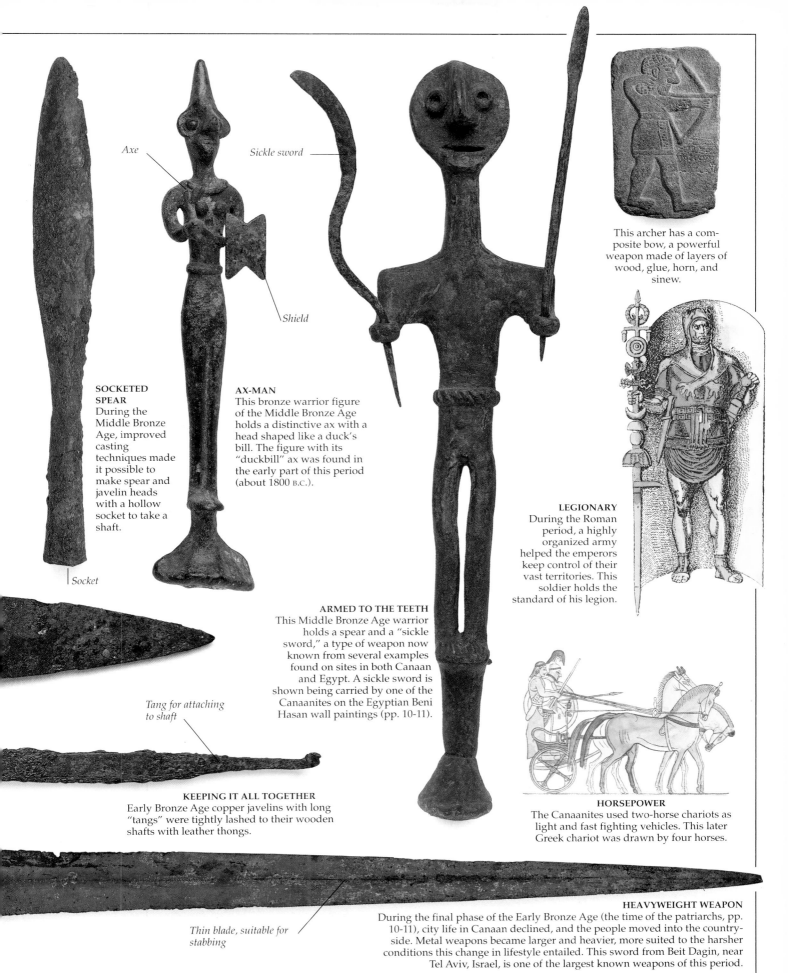

SOCKETED SPEAR
During the Middle Bronze Age, improved casting techniques made it possible to make spear and javelin heads with a hollow socket to take a shaft.

Socket

Axe

Sickle sword

Shield

AX-MAN
This bronze warrior figure of the Middle Bronze Age holds a distinctive ax with a head shaped like a duck's bill. The figure with its "duckbill" ax was found in the early part of this period (about 1800 B.C.).

This archer has a composite bow, a powerful weapon made of layers of wood, glue, horn, and sinew.

LEGIONARY
During the Roman period, a highly organized army helped the emperors keep control of their vast territories. This soldier holds the standard of his legion.

ARMED TO THE TEETH
This Middle Bronze Age warrior holds a spear and a "sickle sword," a type of weapon now known from several examples found on sites in both Canaan and Egypt. A sickle sword is shown being carried by one of the Canaanites on the Egyptian Beni Hasan wall paintings (pp. 10-11).

Tang for attaching to shaft

KEEPING IT ALL TOGETHER
Early Bronze Age copper javelins with long "tangs" were tightly lashed to their wooden shafts with leather thongs.

HORSEPOWER
The Canaanites used two-horse chariots as light and fast fighting vehicles. This later Greek chariot was drawn by four horses.

Thin blade, suitable for stabbing

HEAVYWEIGHT WEAPON
During the final phase of the Early Bronze Age (the time of the patriarchs, pp. 10-11), city life in Canaan declined, and the people moved into the country-side. Metal weapons became larger and heavier, more suited to the harsher conditions this change in lifestyle entailed. This sword from Beit Dagin, near Tel Aviv, Israel, is one of the largest known weapons of this period.

Continued on next page

The siege of Lachish

The northern kingdom of Israel came to an end in 722 B.C. with the capture of its capital, Samaria, by the Assyrians. The southern kingdom of Judah was also forced to submit to the might of the Assyrians, and although Hezekiah (715-686 B.C.) rebelled against the Assyrian king Sennacherib in 704 B.C., the attempt was a disaster. In 701 B.C. Sennacherib swept into Judah and destroyed many cities, including Lachish. The siege and capture of this city are vividly depicted in a series of limestone reliefs from Sennacherib's palace at Nineveh. The Assyrians finally advanced on Jerusalem, where Hezekiah was forced to submit and pay heavy tribute.

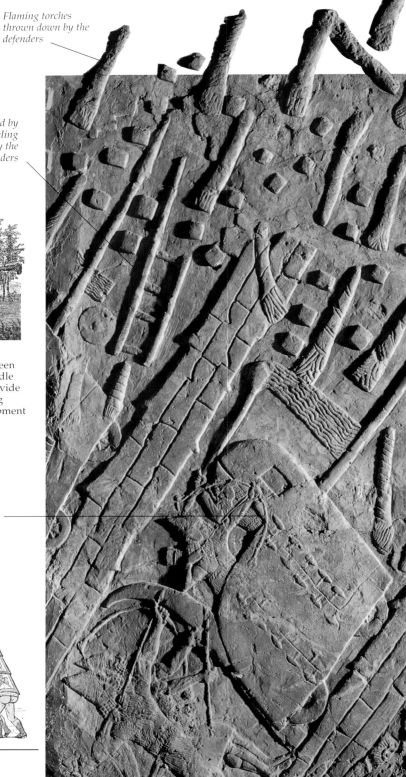

Flaming torches thrown down by the defenders

Broken ladder – used by the Assyrians for scaling but pushed down by the defenders

Battering ram – the soldier at the front is pouring water over the front of the machine so that it won't catch fire

MIGHTY MAN
This painting by 19th-century artist William Dyce shows Joash, son of Shemaah of Gibeah, who was one of David's heroes.

ARROWHEADS
When bronze became freely available after 2000 B.C., arrowheads made of the metal were used widely. Iron arrowheads came in after about 1100 B.C.

Selection of bronze arrowheads

DOWN WITH THE WALLS
The battering ram may have been developed as early as the Middle Bronze Age. It continued to provide an effective way of attacking defensive walls until the development of explosives.

Iron arrowhead

TORTOISE SHELL
The Romans used stout swords and big rectangular shields. In close formations, especially when attacking cities, soldiers would lock their shields together to form a solid wall or roof. This formation was known as a *testudo*, or tortoise.

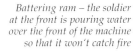

BETTER BATTLE-AXES
During the period of the patriarchs, toward the end of the third millennium B.C., battle-axes were developed that could be secured to the handle by means of a socket. They were highly effective in piercing metal helmets – and cracking skulls!

Ax head with handle

DUCK'S BILL
During the Middle Bronze Age, ax blades were made longer to produce the so-called "duckbill" ax.

Parapet of round shields on top of city gatehouse

Judean archers and slingers defending the gatehouse

Large hooded shield

Assyrian archer – the pointed helmet was effective protection against vertically falling showers of arrows

Assyrian spearman with crested helmet

Siege ramps of banked-up earth covered with logs

Deportees leaving the gate, bound for exile in Assyria, carrying with them a few possessions in bags

Bronze scale armor like this was worn by the Assyrians during the siege of Lachish

A 19th-century impression of scale armor

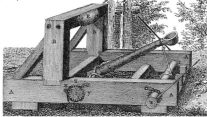

This Roman catapult could hurl rocks over long distances. It was called an *onager* (wild ass) because of its kicking action.

The Assyrians

THE KINGDOM OF ASSYRIA was centered on the valley of the Tigris River in northern Iraq. It had existed since at least 2000 B.C. During the 9th century B.C., the Assyrian kings began to expand their territory, both to secure their boundaries and to gain control of trade routes. The next 200 years saw the relentless advance of the Assyrian armies in regular campaigns against Syria, Phoenicia, and ultimately Israel and Judah. The kings of these states could buy a little time by paying tribute to the Assyrians – taxes in the form of treasures or other goods – but failure to meet the increasing demands, or any form of resistance, was met by crushing retaliation. Territories conquered by the Assyrians were added to the growing empire. In 722 B.C. the northern kingdom of Israel effectively came to an end with the taking of its capital, Samaria, and the loss of part of its population through the Assyrian policy of moving people from their homelands. Judah survived longer, but only by paying crippling tribute. Many of the exploits of the Assyrians are shown on carved stone slabs made to adorn the royal palaces.

HOUSEHOLD GOD
The Assyrians often placed figures of gods beneath the floors of their houses and palaces to keep out evil demons. This one is the god Lahmu, "the hairy."

HEROIC STRUGGLE
In spite of their warlike image, the Assyrians greatly appreciated art and fine craftsmanship. This carved ivory plaque shows a hero or king fighting a lion. It was made locally in Assyria.

THE EMPIRE'S SPREAD
At its greatest extent, in the early 7th century B.C., the Assyrian Empire covered a vast area, stretching from Iran to Egypt.

Nineveh
Nimrud
Damascus
Jerusalem
Memphis
Ur
Susa

Bottle

FOR HOME AND PALACE
These two vessels show the skill and artistry of the Assyrian potter. The elegant, thin-walled beaker on the left is an example of "Assyrian palace ware." On the right is a small bottle, beautifully decorated in multicolored glaze. Both pieces date to the 8th-7th centuries B.C.

Beaker

WAR GODDESS
This bronze plaque shows Ishtar, the most important goddess of the Assyrians. Here she is depicted as the goddess of war, carrying arms and mounted on her favorite animal, the lion. Ishtar was the equivalent of the Canaanite goddess Astarte (pp. 20-21).

TRIBUTE FROM PHOENICIA
Carved ivories were often used to decorate furniture. This panel from the Assyrian capital, Nimrud, showing a woman wearing an Egyptian-style wig, was made by a Phoenician craftworker. It was probably brought back in the 8th century B.C. from one of the western campaigns as part of war booty or tribute.

GODDESS OF LOVE
This blue plaque showing a winged goddess comes from the temple of Ninurta at Nimrud. It dates to the 9th century B.C. The goddess is probably Ishtar, shown in her guise as goddess of love.

Blue color typical of Assyrian decorative wares

PAYMENTS TO THE KING
The military campaigns of the Assyrian king Shalmaneser III (858-824 B.C.) were commemorated on a stone monument, now known as the Black Obelisk, which was set up in the capital, Nimrud. One of the scenes shows Jehu, king of Israel, giving tribute to Shalmaneser. The kneeling figure may not be Jehu himself, but a representative. The tribute itself is shown on another panel.

LION'S SHARE
Lions were a popular subject in Assyrian art. This one might originally have been attached to the handle of a fan.

MAKING YOUR MARK
Small stone cylinders with a hole through them were carved with a design and rolled out on clay tablets or jar or parcel sealings. The resulting impression acted as a signature or mark of ownership. This chalcedony seal, dating to around 750 B.C., shows a heroic figure grasping two ostriches by the neck.

STATEROOM
The richly decorated throne room of King Ashurnasirpal II at Nimrud is shown here reconstructed by a 19th-century artist. The carved reliefs, which today are seen as plain stone, were originally brightly painted.

The Babylonians

Hebrew seal of the Neo-Babylonian period

Mesopotamia, the land between the Tigris and Euphrates rivers in what is now Iraq, was one of the earliest centers of civilization in the Middle East. At the start of the 2nd millennium B.C., the Amorites, a people originally from the Syrian desert, founded a dynasty at the city of Babylon on the Euphrates. In the 18th century B.C., under King Hammurabi, the Babylonians achieved supremacy over the whole of Mesopotamia, establishing an empire that stretched from Mari in the northwest to Elam in the east. This "Old Babylonian" period was brought to an end by the Hittite King Mursilis I, who attacked Babylonia in 1595 B.C. and destroyed the city of Babylon. In the 7th century B.C., the city's fortunes improved when the local official Nabopolassar took control of southern Mesopotamia and assumed kingship of Babylon, founding the Neo-Babylonian dynasty.

Stone maceheads were often dedicated to the gods and placed in temples. This one is dedicated to Nergal, god of disease.

NABOPOLASSAR'S EMPIRE
In 612 B.C., Nabopolassar overthrew the Assyrians and laid claim to their lands, including Judah. His son Nebuchadnezzar raided Judah in 597 B.C. after a rebellion. When revolt broke out again ten years later, Nebuchadnezzar responded with a devastating campaign which destroyed Jerusalem.

BUILDER
Bronze figures showing a king carrying a basket filled with building materials were placed in the foundations of temples. The inscription gives the names of the king and the god of the temple.

AGE OF AQUARIUS
The Babylonians are thought to have invented the zodiac. This terra-cotta plaque shows a giant carrying streams of water – the ancestor of Aquarius.

GREAT GATE
Nebuchadnezzar rebuilt Babylon. One of the most impressive buildings was the Ishtar Gate, which gave access to the processional road leading to the main temple.

TOWER OR TEMPLE? *right*
According to the book of Genesis, the tower of Babel was built by the descendants of Noah in order to reach Heaven. This is a reference to Babylon's ziggurat or temple tower. This depiction of the tower is from a detail of a painting by Pieter Bruegel the elder (1525-1569).

ON THE BOUNDARY
In the Old Babylonian period, allocations of land and tax concessions granted to individuals or districts were recorded on clay tablets. A more public way of recording such agreements was the boundary stone, an elaborately carved and inscribed stone set up in the temple or the field to which the agreement related. The symbols on the stone represent the gods and goddesses who witnessed the contract.

The planet Venus, representing Ishtar, goddess of love and fertility

Snake symbol of the underworld god Ishtaran

Moon, representing the moon god Sin

Sun, representing the sun god Shamash

Nabu, god of writing, seen here as a wedge-shaped (cuneiform) symbol

Scorpion, symbol of the goddess Ishhara

Altars and shrines

The Persians

ORIGINALLY FROM CENTRAL ASIA, the Persians moved into western Iran during the second millennium B.C. and settled in Parsa (now Fars). Their early history is closely linked to that of the Medes, who settled in the same region. In alliance with the Babylonians, the Medes, under their king Cyaxares, overthrew the Assyrian state in 612 B.C. In 550 B.C. Cyrus of the house of Achaemenes deposed his grandfather, the Median king Astyages, and became undisputed ruler of both Medes and Persians. The Achaemenid Empire was born, and began to increase its power. Soon Cyrus had added much of western Anatolia to his territories. In 539 B.C. he defeated Babylonia and inherited its empire, which included Syria and Palestine. It was during the reign of Cyrus that the Jews were allowed to return to Palestine. The rebuilding of Jerusalem and its temple are described in the Books of Ezra and Nehemiah.

Wealthy or important people sewed ornaments like this onto their clothes.

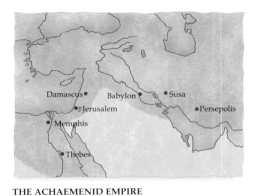

THE ACHAEMENID EMPIRE
At its maximum extent during the reign of Darius I (522-486 B.C.), the empire stretched from Egypt and Libya in the west to the Indus River in the east.

ROYAL CENTER
Persepolis was an important civic and religious center built by Darius I and his successor Xerxes (486-465 B.C.). It is shown here in an imaginative 19th-century reconstruction.

GLAMOROUS GOAT
This silver goat is said to come from Persepolis and dates to the 5th century B.C.

ON GUARD
This Persian palace guard is portrayed on a glazed brick frieze from Susa.

Cuneiform (wedge-shaped) script

LION AT BAY
A royal lion hunt is portrayed on this impression of an agate cylinder seal. The inscription records the name "Darius the Great King," probably Darius I.

Ahuramazda, the supreme god of the Persians

FINERY FROM AFAR
The Persian kings employed artists and craftworkers of many nationalities, and foreign influence can be seen in many of their works of art. The applied golden figures on this silver bowl show a winged lion with the head of the Egyptian dwarf god Bes, wearing a feathered crown.

LIGHT ON THE SUBJECT
Dating to the 6th century B.C., this bronze lamp was found in the "Solar shrine" at Lachish, a small temple associated with sun worship.

Spout to take wick

HIGH CEREMONY
This imaginative reconstruction shows one of the ceremonies that might have taken place at Persepolis.

CYRUS CYLINDER
The text on this clay cylinder tells how Cyrus allowed people in captivity in Babylon to return to their homelands. It does not mention the Jews, but it was this policy that allowed them to return to Palestine.

The Bible as evidence

THE BIBLE AS WE KNOW IT today is not a single book, but a collection of 63 individual books divided into two main parts, the Old and New Testaments. For archeologists working in the Holy Land, the Bible is a major source, containing a wealth of historical, religious, philosophical, socio-logical, literary, and poetic material. But it must, like any other ancient collection of texts, be used critically. Many of the Old Testament books are edited compi-lations, put into their final form a long time after the events they describe. The development of the Bible and the disentangling of the various strands that form its books are fields of study in their own right.

DEAD SEA SCROLLS
In 1947 a goatherd stumbled into a cave at Qumran, Jordan. It contained the ancient Hebrew manuscripts now called the Dead Sea Scrolls. They had been stored in jars like this one. Although incomplete and fragmentary, the scrolls must originally have included all of the books of the Old Testament and Apocrypha. They are the oldest versions of the texts known so far.

One of the Dead Sea Scrolls contains the text of the Book of the prophet Habakkuk, together with a commentary in which the words of the prophet are set against con-temporary events

THE BIBLE IN GREEK
The 4th-century A.D. Codex Sinaiticus is inscribed in Greek capital letters in ink on parchment. It was discovered at St. Catherine's monastery, right.

HIDING PLACE OF THE SCROLLS
Caves in the Judean Desert, close to the Dead Sea, were the hiding places of the Scrolls. They probably came from the library of Qumran, the monastery of the Essenes, a highly religious group of Jews. The scrolls were put in the caves to protect them from the Romans during the first Jewish revolt (p. 45).

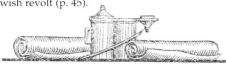

TURIN SHROUD
The Shroud of Turin was long regarded as one of the holiest of Christian relics. It was believed to be the shroud in which Jesus of Nazareth was wrapped following the Crucifixion, and bore an extraordinary image said to be that of Christ himself. Modern scientific testing, using radiocarbon analysis, has since shown that it is in fact a medieval fake.

Jesus asking for the children to be brought to him

MOSAIC MAP
In 1884, a remarkable mosaic was discovered in the Greek Orthodox church in Madaba, Jordan. Dating to the 6th century A.D., it depicts a map of the Holy Land with pictures of towns, individual buildings, and other details. Although parts of the map have suffered considerable damage, it preserves a fine illustration of Jerusalem and parts of the Jordan Valley and the Negev.

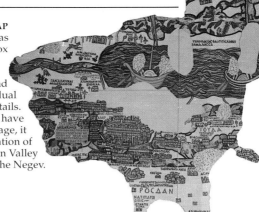

GOSPEL
This page of St. Luke's Gospel is from a 5th-century text, the Codex Alexandrinus.

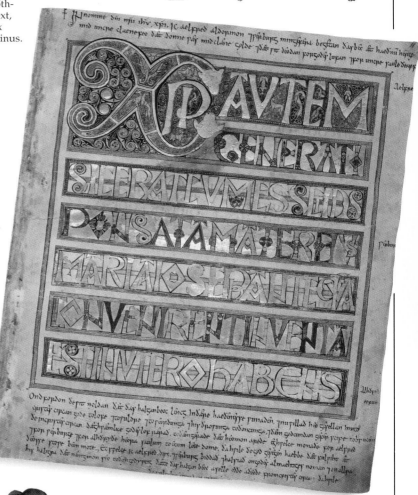

ILLUMINATED MANUSCRIPT
In the medieval period, highly decorated or "illuminated" manuscripts of the Bible were produced by monks. This example is from a Latin Bible of around 750, preserved in the Royal Library in Stockholm, Sweden.

BEFORE THE CRUCIFIXION
This portrayal of Christ wearing the crown of thorns is by the 15th-century Flemish painter Quentin Massys.

Continued on next page

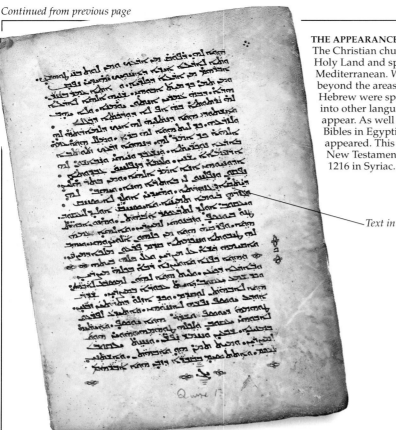

Text in Syriac

THE APPEARANCE OF TRANSLATIONS

The Christian church began in the Holy Land and spread through the Mediterranean. When it spread beyond the areas where Greek and Hebrew were spoken, translations into other languages began to appear. As well as Bibles in Latin, Bibles in Egyptian and Syriac appeared. This manuscript of the New Testament was written in 1216 in Syriac.

MOSES AND THE TABLETS

When Moses returned from Mount Sinai he brought with him stone tablets engraved with the law.

Text in Hebrew

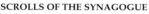

SCROLLS OF THE SYNAGOGUE

Hebrew scribes meticulously copied out the texts of the Old Testament books onto parchment, which was rolled up and kept in the Jewish places of worship, the synagogues.

HEBREW BIBLE

This page from a Hebrew Bible shows the story of the Exodus. This is quite a recent Hebrew Bible, but the text has changed very little since the Dead Sea Scrolls were written out almost 2,000 years ago.

Scrolls covered in fine cloth

JESUS IN THE TEMPLE

The young Jesus was once discovered in discussion with the wise men at the Temple. This story shows the importance of scholarship and debate for the Jews – a tradition which has continued to this day. The episode is shown here in a painting by William Holman Hunt (1827-1910).

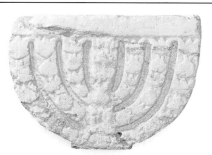

THE MENORAH

The Hebrew word *menorah* means "lampstand." In the Old Testament it refers specifically to the seven-branched candlestick which stood in the Temple of Jerusalem and later became a Jewish symbol. The menorah was removed from the Temple by the Romans in A.D. 70. It is depicted , with other objects similarly looted, in the carvings on the arch of Titus (p. 45).

KING DAVID

David was the second king of Israel. According to the Bible he began his career as a shepherd boy and was the writer of the Psalms. He is shown here in a painting by Pietro Perugino (1446-1524).

THE FIRST PRINTED BIBLE

Johannes Gutenberg was one of the inventors of printing with movable type in the 15th century. His Bible, which appeared in 1456, was the first printed edition. The text was in Latin. Printed texts made the Bible much more accessible. Soon, printed translations of the Bible into the modern European languages started to roll off the press.

Text in Latin

Text in English

THE BIBLE IN ENGLISH

English translations of the Bible began to appear with a version by John Wycliffe in 1384. William Tyndale was the first English translator to tackle the New Testament. His New Testament first appeared in 1526. It had to be smuggled into England because there was so much opposition to translations of the original biblical texts.

An Arab encampment painted by David Roberts (1796-1864)

King Herod

HEROD WAS THE SON OF ANTIPATER, adviser to John Hyrcanus, the last of the Hasmonean rulers. When the Roman general Pompey entered Jerusalem in 63 B.C. and outraged the Jewish community by entering the Holy of Holies (p. 17), Hyrcanus and Antipater were shrewd enough to avoid conflict. They skillfully walked a political tightrope during the power struggle between Julius Caesar and Pompey, changing allegiance to Caesar at just the right time. Herod was clever too, at first backing Mark Antony, then changing to support Antony's victorious rival, Augustus. In this way Herod was seen as a friend of Rome and was rewarded by being made king of Judea in 40 B.C.

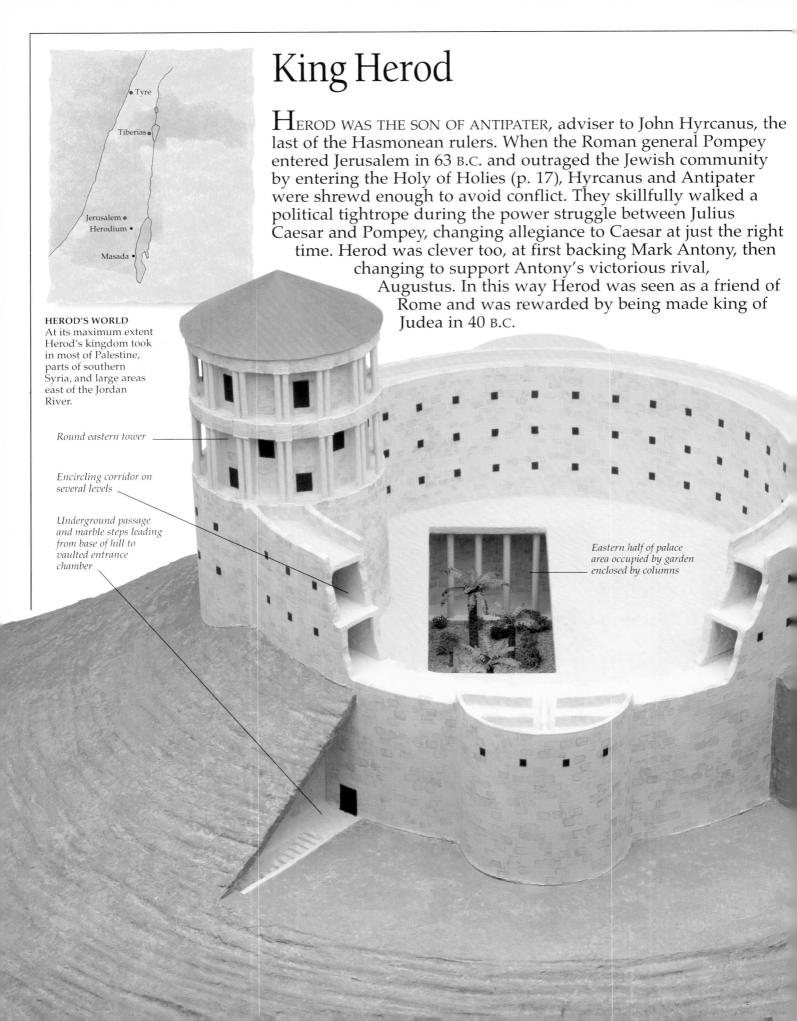

HEROD'S WORLD
At its maximum extent Herod's kingdom took in most of Palestine, parts of southern Syria, and large areas east of the Jordan River.

Round eastern tower

Encircling corridor on several levels

Underground passage and marble steps leading from base of hill to vaulted entrance chamber

Eastern half of palace area occupied by garden enclosed by columns

WILD WOMAN
John the Baptist, whose head was brought to Salome, was a prisoner at Herod's fortress at Machaerus. The story is shown in a detail of a painting by Lucas Cranach (1472-1553).

WELL APPOINTED
The western half of the palace area at Herodium contained living quarters and service rooms. On the north side was this impressive bathhouse. It was richly ornamented with mosaic floors and frescoes (paintings on plaster).

HERODIUM *right and below*
Herod was a great builder. Little has survived of his greatest achievement, the rebuilt Temple at Jerusalem. But excavations of his palatial mountaintop fortress around the Jordan Valley and the Dead Sea have shown something of the splendor of his architecture. Herod's hilltop fortress of Herodium, 7 miles (12 km) south of Jerusalem, is a good example. It contained a luxurious palace and was also Herod's burial place. The picture shows an aerial view of the site today; the model is a reconstruction of what it looked like in Herod's time.

WALL OF TEARS
The Wailing Wall at Jerusalem is part of the western retaining wall of the huge sanctuary that contained Herod's Temple at its center.

Semicircular tower, mostly covered by the artificial hill

Upper part of hill is an artificial rampart encasing the lower parts of the fortress

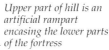

MASSACRE OF THE INNOCENTS
According to the New Testament, it was Herod the Great (Herod I) who was responsible for the slaughter of the children in his attempt to dispose of Jesus of Nazareth. In reality the story is a myth.

MASADA
At Masada, later to become famous during the first Jewish revolt, Herod added to the existing buildings a series of huge water cisterns, storehouses for ammunition and food, and a luxurious palace constructed on three natural rock terraces.

The Greeks and Romans

THE VAST EMPIRE of the Persians was taken over by the Macedonian ruler Alexander the Great in 332 B.C. When Alexander died nine years later, Palestine first came under the control of his general Ptolemy and Ptolemy's descendants, then passed to the rule of the Seleucids, a dynasty based in Syria. In 167 B.C., the Seleucid king Antiochus IV sacked and looted the Temple in Jerusalem and forbade Jewish religious practices. The Jews revolted and, through a series of brilliant military campaigns, were able to defeat the Seleucids and secure a brief period of independence for Judah (about 142-63 B.C.). This period, of the so-called Hasmonean kingdom, was brought to an end by a bitter civil war which was only stopped when Rome, the power that finally drove the Seleucids from Syria, intervened. In 63 B.C. the Roman general Pompey entered Jerusalem. The area, now called Judea, was given semi-independence in 40 B.C., when the Roman senate, in recognition of his loyalty to Rome, appointed Herod king. Herod's son Archelaus succeeded his father in 4 B.C., but he was unsatisfactory as a ruler. In A.D. 6 he was dismissed by the Roman emperor Augustus, leaving Judea as a Roman province, ruled by officials called procurators.

TIME OF CHANGE
Alexander the Great had a vast empire stretching from Greece to western India. The period when Palestine was part of this empire was one of change for the area. Longstanding traditions were overturned in the process of "Hellenism," the full-scale importing of Greek (and later, Roman) culture, including art, architecture, religion, and language.

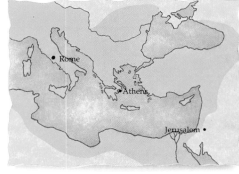

WHERE THE ROMAN WRIT RAN
By the time of the Roman emperor Titus, the entire Mediterranean area was under Roman rule.

FROM GREECE TO EGYPT
When Alexander died, his empire was fought over by his generals. Ptolemy I, a Macedonian, seized Egypt and Palestine, and founded a dynasty that ruled from a new capital, Alexandria, in Egypt. The Ptolemies were Greek but were often portrayed as traditional Egyptian rulers. This painted limestone stela shows Ptolemy II, who succeeded his father in 283 B.C.

PORTABLE ALTAR
This miniature bronze altar of the Roman period comes from Byblos. Once an important Phoenician city and port, Byblos became a minor town in the Roman period.

SACRIFICE TO THE GODS
The enforced worship of pagan Greek and Roman gods and goddesses was deeply resented by the Jews.

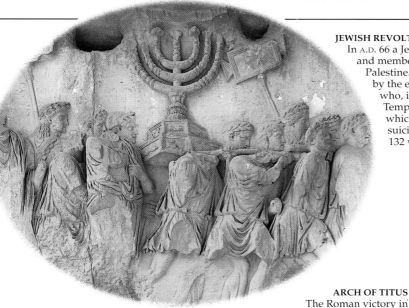

JEWISH REVOLTS

In A.D. 66 a Jewish revolt against Roman rule, led by priests and members of the sect of Pharisees, broke out in Palestine. The revolt was put down with great severity by the emperor Vespasian, together with his son Titus, who, in A.D. 70, captured Jerusalem and destroyed the Temple. The last stronghold of the Jews was Masada, which fell to the Romans in A.D. 74 after the mass suicide of the defenders. A second revolt in A.D. 132 was crushed by the emperor Hadrian.

Marble bust of the Roman emperor Tiberius

ARCH OF TITUS

The Roman victory in the first Jewish war was commemorated in sculpted friezes on a magnificent arch in Rome. The arch was erected by the emperor Domitian in memory of his brother Titus.

CALVARY

After A.D. 6 Judea was a province of the Roman Empire, run by procurators. It was under the fifth procurator, Pontius Pilate (A.D. 27-30), that Jesus Christ was crucified.

CRUCIFIXION

This reconstruction shows how Jesus might have been crucified.

This amusing Roman "face" juglet from Jerusalem was made in a mold. It dates to the 2nd century A.D.

NEW GODS FOR OLD

The Greeks and Romans introduced their own gods and goddesses. In Phoenicia, where Canaanite religion had persisted until the coming of Alexander, most of the new gods could be related to the old gods. The "new" goddess Aphrodite, shown here in a bronze statue from Byblos, was identified with the Canaanite and Phoenician fertility goddess Astarte (pp. 20-21).

ROMAN BURIALS

During the Roman period burial was a two-stage process. After death, the body was wrapped in linen, sprinkled with perfume, and placed on a shelf inside a tomb. After some time, when the flesh had decayed, the relatives would enter the tomb, gather up the bones, and place them in a stone box called an ossuary.

The Greek world

THE BRITISH MUSEUM
The architecture of the British Museum in London was inspired by Classical Greek architecture. The first part of the museum was completed in 1827 and the building as it is today gradually arose over the next 30 years. Many of the objects in this book can be seen there.

THE LAND OF GREECE is made up of mainland Greece and numerous islands scattered throughout the Aegean and Adriatic seas. It is a mountainous country with hot, dry summers and rain only in winter. The early Greek settlements developed as small independent communities cut off from each other by the mountains and often competing for the best land, because fertile soil is in short supply. Each of the "city-states" that developed out of these communities had a strong individual identity, and citizens were loyal to their home state and its patron deity (god). This miscellaneous collection of city-states sometimes joined together for mutual defense, most successfully against the Persians in the 490s and 480s B.C. The Greeks produced a glorious culture, which has had a profound effect on Western civilization through succeeding centuries, right down to the present day. The ancient Greeks scaled the heights in literature, visual and dramatic arts, philosophy, politics, sports, and many other aspects of human life. Greek civilization reached its peak in Athens in the fifth century B.C.

KOUROS
Kouroi (marble statues of naked boys) were made mainly in the sixth century B.C. to decorate sanctuaries of the gods, particularly Apollo, but some may have been put up in memory of young soldiers who had died in battle. They stand with their arms by their sides and one foot in front of the other.

THE ANCIENT GREEK WORLD
This map shows ancient Greece and the surrounding area. It includes towns established by the first emigrants from the mainland who traveled east. The emigrants settled on Ionia, a coastal area of Asia Minor. The names of the regions are in capitals and the cities are in small letters.

DONKEY DRINKING CUP
Beautifully painted pottery was a specialty of the Greeks. It was used mainly for storing, mixing, serving, and drinking wine. This is a special two-handled cup in the form of a donkey's head.

ACROPOLIS
Athens (pp. 58-59) was the most important city of ancient Greece, and the center for all forms of arts and learning. Its Acropolis (fortified hill) was crowned with the temple of the Parthenon, dedicated to the goddess Athena.

HIPPOCAMP
The gold ring is decorated with a hippocamp, a sea horse with two forefeet and a body ending in the tail of a dolphin or a fish.

GREECE AND THE WIDER WORLD
This chart shows the rise and fall of the Greek world from Minoan times (pp. 48-49) to the end of the Hellenistic period. These historic events can be seen against a background of other civilizations in Europe, Asia, and South America.

DATES B.C.	2000–1500	1500–1100	1100–800	800–480	480–323	323–30
EVENTS IN GREECE	Cretan palace (Minoan) civilization.	Fall of Knossos. Rise and fall of Mycenaean civilization.	The foundation of Sparta. The formation of Homeric poems.	Ionian and Black Sea colonies founded. First Olympic Games.	Persian invasions. Start of democracy in Athens. Sparta controls the Peloponnesus. Age of Pericles.	Rise of Macedon. Fall of Sparta. Life of Alexander. Wars of Alexander's successors.
CULTURAL PERIOD	Bronze Age	Bronze Age	Dark Age	Archaic Age	Classical Age	Hellenistic Age
WORLD EVENTS	Indus Valley civilizations in India.	Hittite Empire in Asia. Babylonian Empire. Mayan civilization in Central America. Chang dynasty in China.	Celtic peoples arrive in Britain. Phoenician colonies in Spain. Olmec civilization in Mexico.	Rise of Etruscans in Italy. Kushites invade Egypt. Rome founded. Assyrian Empire.	Confucius born in China. Assyrians conquer lower Egypt. Persian Empire.	Toltecs settle in central Mexico. Ch'in dynasty in China. Great Wall built in China.

MARATHON MEN
Athletics was a favorite pastime in ancient Greece (pp 80-81). Games took place as part of religious festivals. These three runners are painted on a pot that was given as a prize to the winner of the race at the Panathenaic Games held in Athens in honor of Athena (pp. 58-59).

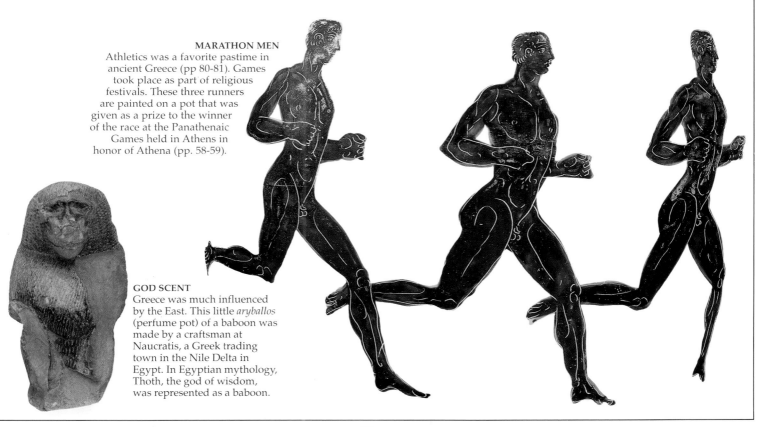

GOD SCENT
Greece was much influenced by the East. This little *aryballos* (perfume pot) of a baboon was made by a craftsman at Naucratis, a Greek trading town in the Nile Delta in Egypt. In Egyptian mythology, Thoth, the god of wisdom, was represented as a baboon.

DECORATING WITH DOLPHINS
The walls of the Minoan palaces were richly decorated with painted scenes known as frescoes, made by applying paint to wet plaster. Many we see today are modern reconstructions based on fragments of painted plaster that have survived. This famous dolphin fresco is from the queen's apartment at Knossos.

Minoan civilization

THE FIRST GREAT CIVILIZATION of the Aegean world flourished on the island of Crete. The area was inhabited as early as 6000 B.C., and the island reached the height of its power between 2200 B.C. and 1450 B.C. Its wealth was a result of its thriving trade with other Bronze Age towns in Greece, the Mediterranean, Egypt, and Syria. Prosperity also came from the rich Cretan soil, which produced oil, grain, and wine grapes in abundance. The economy was based around rich palaces, the remains of which have been found in different parts of the island. This peaceful Cretan civilization is known as Minoan, after a legendary king of Crete called Minos. Knossos and the other palaces were destroyed by fire around 1700 B.C., after which they were rebuilt, even more luxuriously. From then until about 1500 B.C., Minoan civilization was at its height.

WORSHIPER
This bronze figure is in an attitude of worship of the gods.

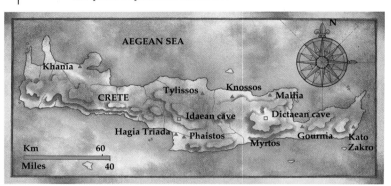

CRETE
This map shows the main towns and palaces on Crete, at Knossos, Zakro, Phaestus, and Mallia. A large villa has also been found at Hagia Triada. Most of the settlements were built close to the sea. The remains of the lavish buildings are evidence of the skill of Minoan architects, engineers, and artists. Not everyone lived in the palaces. Some lived in smaller town houses or in farmhouses in the country. It is said that the young Zeus was brought up in the Dictaean Cave on the high plain of Lassithi.

TAKING THE BULL BY THE HORNS
The bull was regarded by the Minoans as a sacred animal. A Greek myth tells the story of the god Zeus falling in love with a beautiful princess called Europa. Zeus turned himself into a white bull and swam to Crete with Europa on his back. They had three sons, one of whom was Minos, who became the king of Crete. Daring bull sports became a way of worshiping the bull. This bronze figure shows a boy somersaulting over a bull's horns.

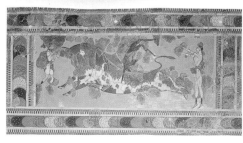

BULL MURAL
This mural at Knossos shows an acrobat leaping over a bull.

DISCOVERING KNOSSOS
English archeologist Sir Arthur Evans discovered the largest of the Minoan palaces at Knossos in 1894. He dug there for several years, and the remains of the colossal building he found, with its hundreds of rooms, amazed the world.

THESEUS AND THE MINOTAUR
According to Greek legend a young prince of Athens called Theseus went to Crete and killed a monster, half-man, half-bull to whom Athenian children were sent as a sacrifice every year.. The monster, the Minotaur, was kept in a maze called the Labyrinth. The huge palace at Knossos has many long, winding corridors; it may have been modeled after the Labyrinth.

MODERN MINOTAUR
The story of the conflict between Theseus and the Minotaur was popular not only with Greek vase painters but also with many modern artists. The interpretation above by Spanish artist Pablo Picasso (1881-1973) is almost as difficult to unravel as the maze!

RESTORATION AND RECONSTRUCTION
The palace of Knossos was made of stone with wooden roofs and ceilings. It was built and rebuilt several times, and some parts of it were four stories high. It had royal apartments, including a throne room where the ruler of Knossos would sit in splendor. Sir Arthur Evans restored some of the palace, so it is now possible to get a sense of what it was like when it was new. The wooden columns are painted the same shade of red as the original stories.

The Mycenaean civilization

GREECE IN THE BRONZE AGE (before iron tools and weapons came into use) had several important centers, including Mycenae. Mycenae, city of the legendary king Agamemnon, was one of several heavily fortified strongholds. The king or chief lived in a palace with many rooms that served as a military headquarters and administrative center for the surrounding countryside. The Mycenaeans were warriors, and weapons and armor have been found in their graves. They were also great traders and sailed far and wide. Their civilization reached its height of power about 1600 B.C. and eclipsed the Minoan civilization of Crete. All seemed secure and prosperous, but around 1250 B.C. the Mycenaeans came under threat from foreign invaders and started to build huge defensive walls around all the major towns. By about 1200 B.C. the cities began to be abandoned or destroyed. Within 100 years the Mycenaean strongholds had fallen and a period often called the Dark Ages had begun.

POMEGRANATE PENDANT
This little gold pendant in the form of a pomegranate was found on the island of Cyprus. It was made by a Mycenaean craftsman around 1300 B.C. and is a good example of a jewelry technique called granulation. Tiny gold granules grouped in triangles decorate its surface. Mycenaean artists and traders settled in Cyprus in large numbers. The island later provided a refuge for many Greeks fleeing from unrest at home as the Mycenaean civilization crumbled.

BULL SPRINKLER
This clay bull's head was used as a ritual sprinkler at religious ceremonies. There are small holes in the mouth to let the water escape. These sprinklers are sometimes in the shape of other animals, but bulls are the most common.

OCTOPUS JAR
This pottery jar with a painting of an octopus was found in a cemetery at a Mycenaean colony on the island of Rhodes. Mycenaean artists were much influenced by Minoan work, and subjects like this, inspired by the sea, continued to be popular.

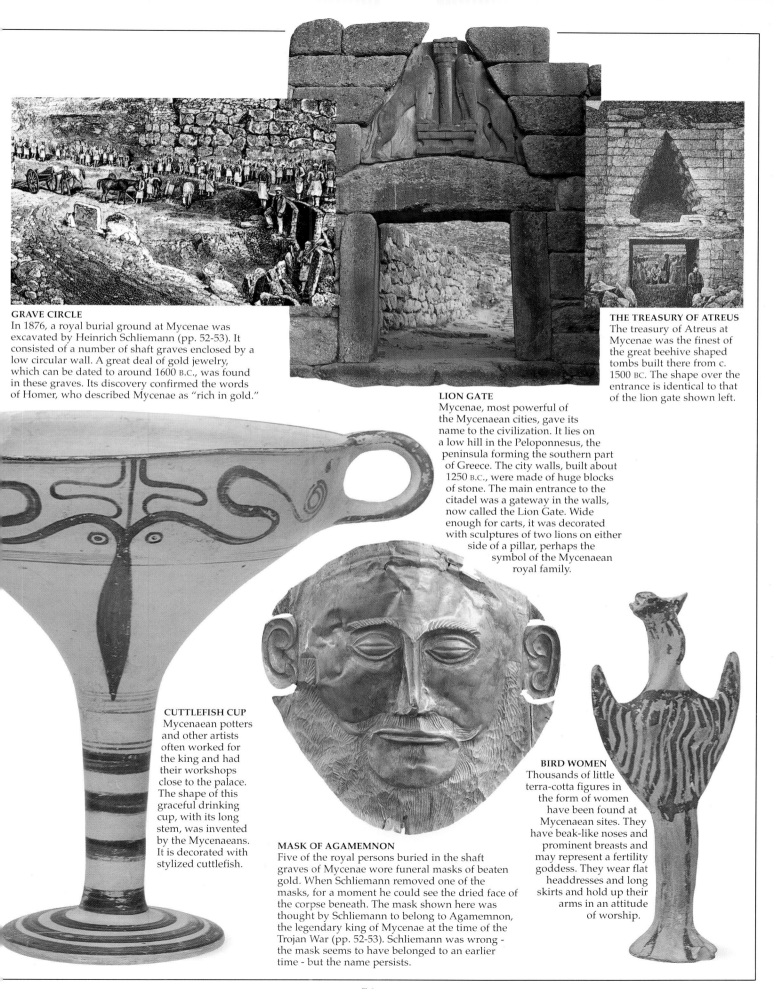

GRAVE CIRCLE
In 1876, a royal burial ground at Mycenae was excavated by Heinrich Schliemann (pp. 52-53). It consisted of a number of shaft graves enclosed by a low circular wall. A great deal of gold jewelry, which can be dated to around 1600 B.C., was found in these graves. Its discovery confirmed the words of Homer, who described Mycenae as "rich in gold."

THE TREASURY OF ATREUS
The treasury of Atreus at Mycenae was the finest of the great beehive shaped tombs built there from c. 1500 BC. The shape over the entrance is identical to that of the lion gate shown left.

LION GATE
Mycenae, most powerful of the Mycenaean cities, gave its name to the civilization. It lies on a low hill in the Peloponnesus, the peninsula forming the southern part of Greece. The city walls, built about 1250 B.C., were made of huge blocks of stone. The main entrance to the citadel was a gateway in the walls, now called the Lion Gate. Wide enough for carts, it was decorated with sculptures of two lions on either side of a pillar, perhaps the symbol of the Mycenaean royal family.

CUTTLEFISH CUP
Mycenaean potters and other artists often worked for the king and had their workshops close to the palace. The shape of this graceful drinking cup, with its long stem, was invented by the Mycenaeans. It is decorated with stylized cuttlefish.

MASK OF AGAMEMNON
Five of the royal persons buried in the shaft graves of Mycenae wore funeral masks of beaten gold. When Schliemann removed one of the masks, for a moment he could see the dried face of the corpse beneath. The mask shown here was thought by Schliemann to belong to Agamemnon, the legendary king of Mycenae at the time of the Trojan War (pp. 52-53). Schliemann was wrong - the mask seems to have belonged to an earlier time - but the name persists.

BIRD WOMEN
Thousands of little terra-cotta figures in the form of women have been found at Mycenaean sites. They have beak-like noses and prominent breasts and may represent a fertility goddess. They wear flat headdresses and long skirts and hold up their arms in an attitude of worship.

To Troy and back

IN THE 12TH CENTURY B.C., the rich Mycenaean towns and palaces fell into decline or were destroyed, trade with the East decreased, and Greece entered a dark age. During the next few centuries, stories of the great Mycenaean civilization that had gone before were handed down from one generation to the next in the form of poems. Two of them, *The Iliad* and *The Odyssey,* have survived. They reached their final form in the eighth century B.C. at the hands of the poet Homer, whose poetry was admired throughout the Greek world. *The Iliad* describes how a city called Troy, on the west coast of modern Turkey, was besieged by a Greek army led by King Agamemnon of Mycenae. It describes the heroic deeds of Greek and Trojan soldiers like Achilles and Hektor. *The Odyssey* tells the story of the return home from the Trojan War of one Greek hero, Odysseus. It took him ten years and he had many adventures along the way. The Homeric stories reflect real incidents of wars, battles, and sieges from an earlier age. It is probable that war was waged between the Greeks and the Trojans, possibly over the ownership of lands and crops at a time when the Mycenaean world was falling apart, and not over the recapture of Helen (above).

HEINRICH SCHLIEMANN
In 1870, German archaeologist Heinrich Schliemann (1822–1890) discovered the site of ancient Troy near the Mediterranean coast in modern Turkey. He had been looking for it for many years. His excavations revealed not just one city, but more than nine of them, built on top of each other. (It is not certain which layer is the city described in *The Iliad*.) Frau Schliemann is wearing some of the superb jewelry found at Troy.

HELEN OF TROY
Helen was the beautiful wife of Menelaus, king of Sparta and brother of Agamemnon, king of Mycenae. According to legend, Helen's capture by Paris, son of Priam, who was king of Troy, caused the Trojan War. The Greeks united to defeat the Trojans and restore Helen to her husband.

OVERCOME BY CURIOSITY
Troy withstood the Greeks' siege for ten long years. In the end, the Greeks triumphed by a trick. They constructed a huge wooden horse, which they left just outside the city. The Trojans then watched the Greek army sail away and, overcome with curiosity, dragged the horse inside the city walls. Late that night, Greek soldiers, hidden inside the horse, crept out and opened the city gates. The Greek army, which had silently returned, entered and destroyed the city. This picture of the horse comes from a pot of about 650–600 B.C.

MODERN MODEL
In Troy today, there is a modern replica of the Trojan horse. It is very large and, like the ancient one, is made of wood. Children can climb a ladder into its stomach and pretend to be Greek soldiers.

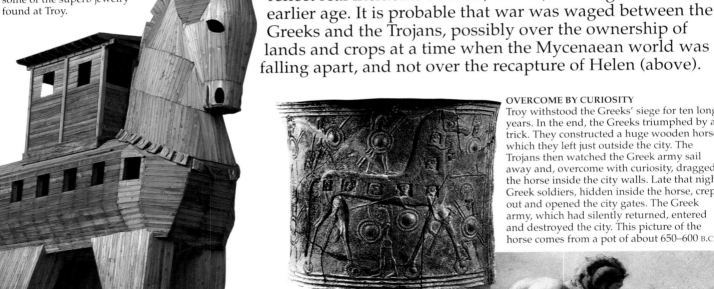

THE WOODEN HORSE
The story of Troy and the wooden horse has been a favorite with artists through the centuries. Italian artist Giovanni Tiepolo (1696–1770) painted more than one version of the subject.

THE BLINDING OF POLYPHEMUS

In one of his adventures on his way home from the Trojan War, the hero Odysseus met a Cyclops called Polyphemus, a man-eating giant with only one eye, in the middle of his forehead. Odysseus and his men were trapped in Polyphemus' cave and the giant started to eat them one by one. Cunning Odysseus brought the giant a skin full of wine, which lulled him into a drunken sleep. Then he blinded Polyphemus by driving a red-hot stake into his only eye.

PATIENT PENELOPE

After his ten-year journey, Odysseus returned at last to Ithaca, his island home, and to his wife, Penelope. During his long absence, she had waited patiently for him, even though everyone else had given him up for dead. When other men proposed marriage to Penelope, she told them that she would give them an answer when she had finished weaving a particular piece of cloth. At night, Penelope crept secretly to her loom and undid everything she had woven during the day. In this way, she postponed indefinitely her reply to her suitors. In this painting by British artist John Stanhope (1829–1908), Penelope is sitting sadly beside her loom.

WOOLLY ESCAPE

Polyphemus kept a flock of sheep in the cave at night and these provided a means of escape. Odysseus and his men tied themselves underneath the sheep. In the morning, the flock filed out of the cave to graze. The blind giant felt the backs of the sheep in case his captives were hiding there, but he did not think to look under their bellies. This story has been illustrated on a black-figure vase.

Blue paint indicating sea

Helmet

MOTHER TO THE RESCUE

The mother of Achilles was a sea nymph called Thetis. This little terra-cotta figurine shows Thetis or one of her sisters riding the waves on a sea horse, bringing a new helmet for Achilles to wear in battle. Some of the bright blue paint, representing the sea, still survives.

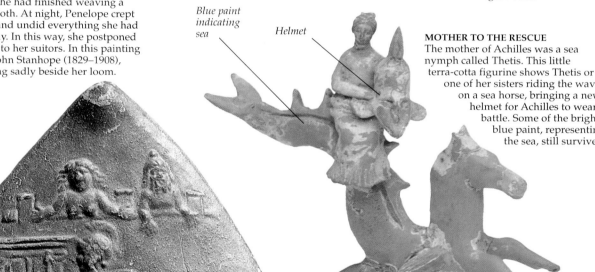

DEATH OF A HERO

After the Greek champion Achilles had killed the bravest Trojan warrior, Hektor, he tied Hektor's body to a chariot and dragged it three times around the walls of Troy. On this clay lamp, Achilles can be seen driving the chariot and looking back in triumph. Above him, on the walls of Troy, Hektor's parents, King Priam and Queen Hecuba, watch in horror.

The state of Sparta

HARBOR BATTLE
The Piraeus is the port of Athens, 4 miles (6 km) to the southwest of the city. In this engraving it is being besieged by Spartan ships in 388 B.C.

SPARTA, IN SOUTHERN GREECE, WAS FOUNDED in the tenth century B.C. by the Dorians, who defeated the original inhabitants of the area. Two centuries later, Sparta conquered its neighbor, Messenia, and gained excellent agricultural land. It became a luxury-loving state producing fine crafts. Music and poetry also flourished. Later the Spartans were defeated in war, and the conquered Messenians engaged in a long-running rebellion, so Sparta turned to military matters. It became a superpower in Greece and the main rival of Athens, and Spartan society was dominated by the need to maintain power. All men of Spartan birth had to serve in the army. Their whole lives were dedicated to learning the arts of war. Boys of seven were taken from their families to live in army barracks. Non-citizens in Sparta were either *perioikoi* or *helots*. The *perioikoi* were free men who, although they did not have the rights of citizens, were allowed to trade and serve in the army. *Helots* were the descendants of the original inhabitants of the area. They farmed the land and did the heavy work for their Spartan overlords.

NATURAL PROTECTION
This 19th-century German engraving shows the site of Sparta in a fertile plain of Lakonia in southern Greece. Its remoteness was an advantage to the warring Spartans, and the high mountains to the east, north, and west, and the sea to the south, formed natural defenses.

SPARTAN WARRIOR
The Greek historian Herodotus wrote that Spartan soldiers, like this one of the fifth century B.C., always combed their long hair when they felt they might be about to put their lives at risk, as when going into battle. The scarlet color of the military cloaks became a symbol of Spartan pride.

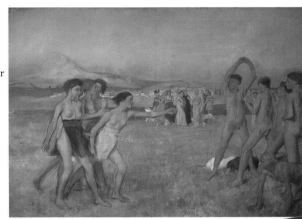

THE YOUNG SPARTANS
Spartan scenes were a popular subject with artists of the 19th century. This unusual painting by the French Impressionist painter Edgar Degas (1834–1917) shows boys and girls exercising in the valley of the Eurotas River, which runs through Sparta. The girls look much more aggressive than girls from other Greek cities.

SPARTAN REGIME
The Spartan system of education, with its emphasis on physical fitness, was much admired in 19th-century England. Corporal (physical) punishment too was regarded as character-forming for schoolboys, just as it was in ancient Sparta. The violence in this cartoon by British cartoonist George Cruikshank (1792–1878) suggests that he thought otherwise.

OFFERINGS

Thousands of small figurines have been found at a sanctuary of Artemis Orthia on the banks of the Eurotas River at Sparta. Among animals such as stags, dogs, and horses are representations of Artemis herself. There are also figurines of the goddess Athena wearing a helmet. The figurines were made at the sanctuary and sold to visitors, who often left them behind as offerings to the goddess. It was to this sanctuary that Spartan boys were taken to be whipped as a demonstration of their toughness and endurance.

Artemis

Warrior

Artemis

Figure playing pipes

IN THE LEAD

This girl is taking part in a running race and is looking back to see how far she is in the lead. She is wearing a very short skirt, which no girl from any other Greek city would dare to wear. Girls did not fight in wars but, like most boys, they were trained in running and for an outdoor life. This made them fit and strong so that they would have healthy babies who would grow up to be good soldiers.

A stag

Greek expansion

GREECE STARTED TO EMERGE from the Dark Ages in the eighth century B.C. Trading posts began to be established abroad, as far away as the Nile Delta in Egypt. As the population expanded and Greek agriculture could no longer meet the needs of the people, some towns sent out colonies both east- and westward. They settled in southern Italy, Sicily, and other parts of the western Mediterranean, and in the East around the shores of the Black Sea. Some of these colonies were very rich. It was said that the people of Sybaris in southern Italy slept on beds of rose petals, and roosters were banned from the town so that the inhabitants would not be woken too early in the morning. Greek culture was influenced by foreign styles. The Geometric style, which, as its name suggests, was dominated by geometric patterns, gave way to a new, so-called Orientalizing style. Designs influenced by the East, such as griffins and sphinxes, were introduced. Egypt and Syria were the main sources. Corinth, Rhodes, and Ephesus were well placed for Eastern trade and became rich.

GOLDEN GRIFFINS
These gold griffin heads, inspired by the East, were found on the island of Rhodes. They were made in the seventh century B.C. and were once attached to a pair of earrings.

MAN SIZE
The Greeks liked to wear bangles decorated with animal heads. This lion-headed bangle, which is silver-plated, may have been worn by a man.

FOND FAREWELL
This detail is from a large pot decorated in the Geometric style. The rigid figures are painted in silhouette. The man on the right is leaving the woman and stepping onto a boat. Perhaps he is meant to be the hero Odysseus saying goodbye to his wife, Penelope, before he goes off to the Trojan War (pp. 52-53), or possibly he is Paris abducting Helen.

LION *ARYBALLOS*
This *aryballos* (perfume pot), which probably came from Thebes, has a spout in the shape of a lion's head. In spite of its small size, it has three zones of painted figures upon it. A horse race can be seen, along with warriors walking in procession. At the bottom is a tiny scene of dogs chasing hares. The mouth of this pot would have been filled with wax to prevent the evaporation of the perfume inside.

FAIENCE FROG
At this time in Greek history, there was much interest in Egyptian art, and the craftsman who made this may have been copying Egyptian work. It shows a man kneeling and holding a jar on top of which is a frog, a sacred creature in Egyptian religion. The object is made of faience, a greenish material often used to make Egyptian ornaments.

EXOTIC EXPORTS
Many little perfume pots were made in the town of Corinth and exported all over the Greek world. They are often in curious shapes and prettily decorated. The winged figure painted on this one may represent a god of the wind.

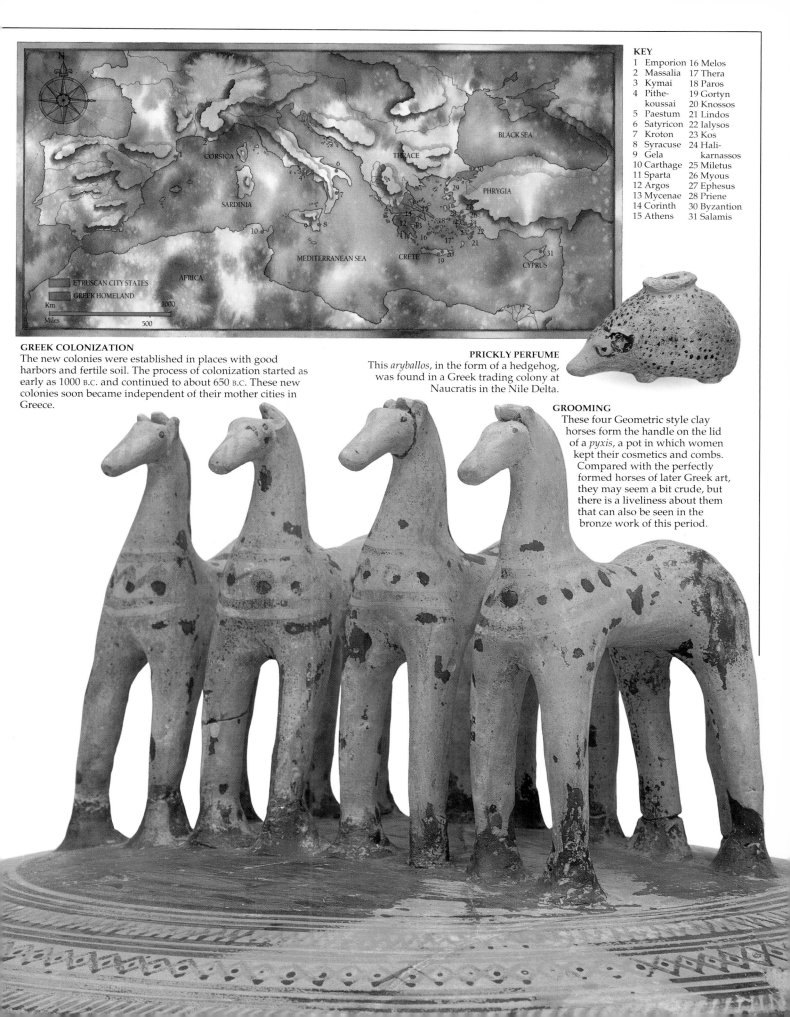

KEY

1	Emporion	16	Melos
2	Massalia	17	Thera
3	Kymai	18	Paros
4	Pithe-	19	Gortyn
	koussai	20	Knossos
5	Paestum	21	Lindos
6	Satyricon	22	Ialysos
7	Kroton	23	Kos
8	Syracuse	24	Hali-
9	Gela		karnassos
10	Carthage	25	Miletus
11	Sparta	26	Myous
12	Argos	27	Ephesus
13	Mycenae	28	Priene
14	Corinth	30	Byzantion
15	Athens	31	Salamis

GREEK COLONIZATION
The new colonies were established in places with good harbors and fertile soil. The process of colonization started as early as 1000 B.C. and continued to about 650 B.C. These new colonies soon became independent of their mother cities in Greece.

PRICKLY PERFUME
This *aryballos*, in the form of a hedgehog, was found in a Greek trading colony at Naucratis in the Nile Delta.

GROOMING
These four Geometric style clay horses form the handle on the lid of a *pyxis*, a pot in which women kept their cosmetics and combs. Compared with the perfectly formed horses of later Greek art, they may seem a bit crude, but there is a liveliness about them that can also be seen in the bronze work of this period.

Athens, city of Athena

THE ACROPOLIS
In early times, the Acropolis (high city) of Athens was a fortified citadel. Later, it became the most sacred part of the town and the site of many important temples and sanctuaries.

SACRED STATUE
The purpose of the procession shown on this frieze (sculptured panel) was to bring a new dress for a sacred wooden statue of Athena at the Acropolis. The dress, a woven *peplos*, is being handed to a priest.

ATHENS WAS THE MOST POWERFUL of all the Greek city-states. It was also a great center of the arts and learning. Its patron, Athena was goddess of wisdom and warfare and perfectly symbolized the two sides of her city's life. In 480 B.C., the Persians invaded and destroyed the city, including the temples on the Acropolis. Later, when Athens had played a leading role in the Persian wars (pp. 82–83) and successfully defended Greece, a huge rebuilding program was launched by the leader of Athens, Perikles.

Athens was situated in an area called Attica and was more densely populated than other Greek cities. The people of Athens lived on the land below the Acropolis. Many fine public squares and colonnaded buildings have been found there around the agora, an open space for meeting and commercial activity. Nearby was the port of Athens, the Piraeus. Access to the sea was a main reason for Athens' military and economic success.

THE ERECHTHEION
A smaller temple than the Parthenon, the Erechtheion, named after a legendary king of Athens, probably housed the wooden statue of Athena. Its famous porch has marble statues of women (*caryatids*), instead of columns, holding up the roof.

THE PARTHENON FRIEZE
The marble frieze of the Parthenon went around all four sides of the temple and was set up high, on the outside of the main building near the ceiling of the colonnade.

Its main subject was the procession of worshipers which wound its way up from the *agora* to the Acropolis every four years as part of the festival called the Great Panathenaea in honor of the goddess Athena. Young men on horseback take up much of the frieze.

THE PARTHENON

The temple of the Parthenon occupies the highest point of the Acropolis. It was dedicated to Athena. The word Parthenon comes from the Greek word *parthenos,* meaning virgin. Athena was sometimes described as Athena Parthenos. The Parthenon, which still stands today, was built between 447 and 432 B.C. The sculptures that decorated it were designed by Pheidias.

GOLDEN GODDESS

Inside the Parthenon stood a huge gold and ivory statue of the goddess Athena, made by the famous sculptor Pheidias, a close friend of Perikles. She appears in all her splendor as goddess of warfare. In this replica based on a smaller copy of the original statue and on descriptions by Greek writers, she wears her *aegis,* a small goatskin cloak fringed with snakes, and a high-crested helmet. On her right hand is a small winged figure of Nike, the goddess of victory.

An Athenian coin showing an owl, the bird of Athena

THE ELGIN MARBLES

Many of the sculptures from the Parthenon were brought to England by Lord Elgin, the British ambassador to the Ottoman court. He saw the sculptures when he visited Athens and was granted permission to bring some back to England. They can be seen today in the British Museum.

Temporary Elgin Room, painted by A. Archer, at the British Museum

Some young men are trotting gently along, and others are galloping with their cloaks flying out behind them. The background to the frieze was originally painted, probably a bright blue. The horses used to have bridles of bronze.

The bridles have not survived, leaving only traces of the holes where they were attached to the marble. In the south frieze a number of young cows can be seen. In other parts of the frieze are women carrying sacrificial vessels, bowls, and jugs.

Gods, goddesses, and heroes

THE GREEKS BELIEVED that all the gods were descendants of Gaia (the earth) and Uranos (the sky). They thought the gods were probably much like humans: they fell in love with each other, married, quarreled, had children, played music, and in many other ways mirrored human characteristics (or humans mirrored theirs). All the gods had their own spheres of influence. Demeter and Persephone were responsible for the grain growing, Artemis was the goddess of hunting, Apollo could foretell the future, and Aphrodite was the goddess of love. Many of the best-known gods had temples and sanctuaries dedicated to them, and much money and artistic ability were lavished on these places. Religion played a large part in the lives of ordinary people. Indeed, most of the beautiful buildings that still survive are temples. Worshipers believed that the gods would treat them well and meet their needs if they offered them animal sacrifices and the fruits of the harvest.

DIONYSOS FROM DELOS
Dionysos was the god of wine and earth fertility. In this mosaic from the island of Delos, he is riding a tiger.

THE KING OF THE GODS
Zeus was the king of the gods. He usually appears in art as a strong, middle-aged, bearded man of great power and dignity. Sometimes he carries his symbol, a thunderbolt.

HOME OF THE GODS
Mount Olympus is the highest mountain in Greece and was believed to be the home of the gods. It is in the north of Greece, on the borders of Thessaly and Macedonia.

GODDESS OF LOVE
This bronze head of Aphrodite comes from eastern Turkey. The goddess was born from the sea foam and believed to have been carried by the Zephyrs (West Winds) to Cyprus. Although she was married to Hephaistos, she fell in love with Ares, the god of war.

BEAUTY AND THE BEAST
On this mirror case, the goddess Aphrodite is playing a game of knucklebones with the god Pan. The goddess of love and beauty is often shown by artists as a graceful young woman, with the upper part of her body bare. She is accompanied by Eros (according to some myths, her son), shown here as a small, winged boy, and a goose, a symbol associated with her. Pan was a god of the countryside and had goat's legs and ears.

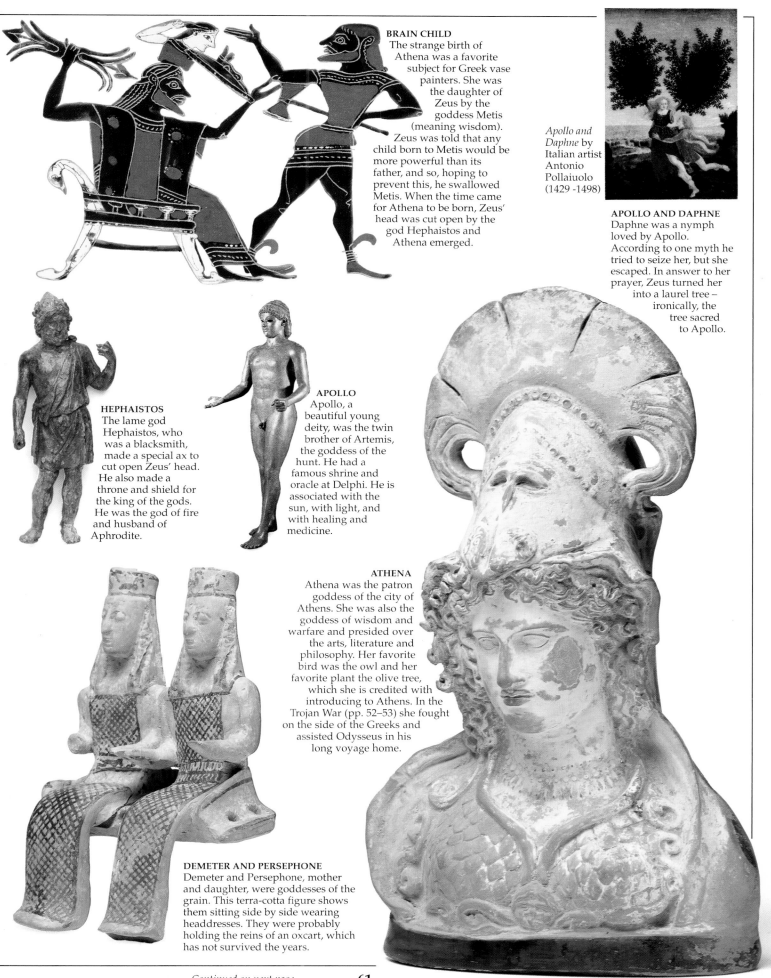

BRAIN CHILD
The strange birth of Athena was a favorite subject for Greek vase painters. She was the daughter of Zeus by the goddess Metis (meaning wisdom). Zeus was told that any child born to Metis would be more powerful than its father, and so, hoping to prevent this, he swallowed Metis. When the time came for Athena to be born, Zeus' head was cut open by the god Hephaistos and Athena emerged.

Apollo and Daphne by Italian artist Antonio Pollaiuolo (1429 -1498)

APOLLO AND DAPHNE
Daphne was a nymph loved by Apollo. According to one myth he tried to seize her, but she escaped. In answer to her prayer, Zeus turned her into a laurel tree – ironically, the tree sacred to Apollo.

HEPHAISTOS
The lame god Hephaistos, who was a blacksmith, made a special ax to cut open Zeus' head. He also made a throne and shield for the king of the gods. He was the god of fire and husband of Aphrodite.

APOLLO
Apollo, a beautiful young deity, was the twin brother of Artemis, the goddess of the hunt. He had a famous shrine and oracle at Delphi. He is associated with the sun, with light, and with healing and medicine.

ATHENA
Athena was the patron goddess of the city of Athens. She was also the goddess of wisdom and warfare and presided over the arts, literature and philosophy. Her favorite bird was the owl and her favorite plant the olive tree, which she is credited with introducing to Athens. In the Trojan War (pp. 52–53) she fought on the side of the Greeks and assisted Odysseus in his long voyage home.

DEMETER AND PERSEPHONE
Demeter and Persephone, mother and daughter, were goddesses of the grain. This terra-cotta figure shows them sitting side by side wearing headdresses. They were probably holding the reins of an oxcart, which has not survived the years.

Continued on next page   **61**

EROS AND PSYCHE

Greek myths were a mixture of stories about gods and heroes. The stories grew with the telling, and there were many different versions. Gods and heroes gained or lost popularity at different periods of Greek history. This Hellenistic terra-cotta piece shows Eros, the god who makes people fall in love, kissing Psyche, the goddess who represents the soul. To the ancient Greeks, their embrace symbolized perfect happiness.

THE FAUN

In this painting by the Italian artist Piero di Cosimo (1462–1521), a woman lies dead, mourned by a faun and a dog. Fauns were identified with the god Pan, who was the protector of shepherds and their flocks.

HERAKLES

The greatest hero of all, Herakles, was the son of Zeus by a mortal woman. As a tiny baby Herakles proved he was a hero by strangling with his bare hands two snakes sent to attack him. In adult life, he performed twelve famous Labors (tasks) for a king named Eurystheus. In the first Labor, Herakles killed the Nemean lion, and is often shown, as on this vase, wearing its skin. The Labor shown here is the killing of the Stymphalian birds. These birds, which lived near a lake in the northeast Peloponnesus, destroyed crops and wounded people with their poisonous feathers. Herakles scared them with a bronze rattle given to him by the smith god Hephaestus (pp. 60–61) and then shot them with a sling. He was strong and fierce but he liked wine and women and had many love affairs.

TOO HIGH!
Icarus was the son of Daedalus, a mythical craftsman who made wings for himself and his son, to enable them to fly. The wings were attached by wax. Icarus flew too high, the heat of the sun melted the wax, and he fell into the Aegean Sea and drowned.

THE BUILDING OF THE ARGO

This Roman terra-cotta wall panel shows a scene from the famous myth of Jason and the Argonauts. Jason was a prince from Thessaly in northern Greece, and the Argonauts were a group of heroes who sailed with him on a ship they had built called the Argo. Heroes are concerned with undertaking long and difficult journeys and freeing mankind from evil, often in the form of strange monsters. Jason and his crew set sail to find the Golden Fleece, which hung on a tree near the Black Sea, guarded by a snake. The goddess Athena helped Jason in this task; she can be seen on the left helping the crew to construct the Argo.

LURE OF THE LYRE

Orpheus was a poet and a musician. He played the lyre and the kithara and sang so well that he could tame wild animals; trees and plants would bend their branches to him, and he could soothe the most violent of tempers. He took part in the expedition of Jason and the Argonauts and calmed the crew and stilled the waves with his music. In this beautiful painting by Dutch artist Roelandt Savery (1576–1639), the magic of Orpheus' music is illustrated. All the birds and beasts are lying down together in an enchanted landscape.

PERSEUS AND MEDUSA

On this vase painting of 460 B.C., the hero Perseus has just cut off the head of the gorgon Medusa. Medusa sinks to the ground with blood spurting from her severed neck. Her head can be seen in Perseus's bag.

Festivals and oracles

RELIGION PLAYED A MAJOR PART in Greek life. The Greeks believed that they could strike a bargain with the gods and offered them gold, silver, and animal sacrifice. They also held festivals and games in their honor. In return, they expected the gods to protect them from illness, look after their crops, and grant other favors. Communication with the gods had a regular place in the calendar; most festivals took place once a year, or sometimes every four years. Gods were worshiped in sanctuaries. One of the most important in Greece was that of Apollo at Delphi. He was associated with light and healing, but if he was angry, his arrows could cause plague. He was well known as a god of prophecy, and at Delphi he would reply to questions about the future. His priestess would act as his mouthpiece and make obscure pronouncements that could be interpreted in different ways. The oracle (as these forecasts were called) at Delphi lasted into Christian times.

COME DANCING
At a festival in the countryside, a row of people join hands and approach an altar where a sacrifice is blazing. A priestess, or perhaps Demeter, the corn goddess, stands behind the altar with a flat basket used for winnowing grain.

HOLY BULL
A bull was one of the animals offered at important sacrificial occasions. Bulls would be decorated with garlands of plants and ribbons to show that they had been set aside for the gods. Garlanded bulls' heads were the inspiration for some of the decorative patterns on temples.

SOMETHING OLD, SOMETHING NEW
The huge columns of a Greek temple at ancient Poseidonia (Paestum) in southern Italy frame a bride and groom posing for their wedding photos. Ancient ruins like these are believed to bring good luck to a new marriage.

CENTER OF THE WORLD
Delphi was thought to be the center of the world, at the very point where two birds flying from opposite ends of the earth met. The Greeks placed a huge stone there, the *omphalos*, or navel of the world. Carved on this version, which is in the museum at Delphi, is a network of woolen strands – a sign that this was a holy object.

TEMPLE OF APOLLO
Delphi was the home of the main shrine of Apollo. It lies on the steep slopes of Mount Parnassus, the favorite haunt of Apollo and also of the Muses, who looked after the arts and music. A road lined with small buildings (to house the rich gifts made to the god) still winds its way up the slope and past the remains of his great temple, which housed the oracle.

SANCTUARY OF ATHENA
The sanctuary of Athena lies farther down the mountain from Apollo's shrine. In the middle of it is this circular building, the purpose of which is unknown. It is set against the silvery blue background of thousands of olive trees. Athena was supposed to have created the olive tree, and these groves still provide a rich harvest for the local people.

THE CHARIOTEER
A stadium was built high above the temple to Apollo at Delphi, for games and chariot races in honor of the god. Winning the chariot race was the greatest honor of the games, and the owner of the winning team of horses paid for a statue to celebrate his success.
The eyes of this magnificent bronze statue are inlaid with glass and stone, the lips are copper, and the headband is patterned with silver. The charioteer is still holding the reins of his horses, even though they have long disappeared. This is one of the best-known statues of ancient Greece.

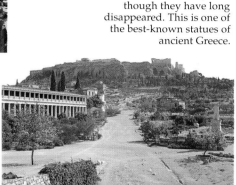

THE WAY TO ATHENA
In the goddess Athena's own city of Athens lay the Panathenaic Way, a special road that led up to her temples and altars on the Acropolis. Leading up from the *agora*, the market and meeting place of the city, the road today passes the rebuilt version of a *stoa*, a long, colonnaded building. It was used for commerce and conversation.

PROCESSION OF SACRIFICE
On this broad bowl used for wine (the ivy leaves that decorate it are linked with Dionysos, the wine god), a long line of people are on their way to worship the goddess Athena. The altar where the flames are already rising is on the right of the bowl. Athena is standing behind the altar. The procession is led by a woman carrying a tray of cakes on her head. She is followed by a man leading the sacrificial bull, then a man playing the double pipes. The rest of the men in the procession carry all the objects necessary for the worship of the goddess, such as a jug of wine. A mule cart brings up the rear.

Temples

GREEK LIFE WAS DOMINATED by religion, so it is not surprising that the temples of ancient Greece were the biggest and most beautiful buildings. They also had a political purpose, as they were often built to celebrate civic power and pride or to offer thanks to the patron deity of a city for success in war. Temples were made of limestone or marble, with roofs and ceilings of wood. Roof tiles were made of terra cotta or stone. Large numbers of workers must have been employed in temple construction. Huge stone blocks had to be transported from quarries in ox-drawn carts. These blocks were carved on site by masons using hammers and mallets. The tall columns were made in cylindrical sections ("drums"), held together with metal pegs and lifted into position with ropes and pulleys. Decorative sculpture in the form of friezes and statues in the pediments (the triangular gable ends), added to the grandeur and beauty of Greek temples.

CAPE SOUNION
A fifth-century marble temple to Poseidon, god of the sea, crowns a high promontory south of Athens. It was a landmark for sailors returning home to Athens. The English romantic poet George Gordon, Lord Byron (1788–1824) was very moved by its beauty.

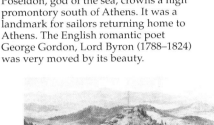

ZEUS'S TEMPLE
A great international festival of athletics (pp. 80–81) in honor of Zeus was held every four years at Olympia, a sanctuary on the banks of the Alpheios river. Colossal remains of the great temple of Zeus built in the fifth century, and other important buildings, have been found there.

TEMPLE OF CERES
Poseidonia (later called Paestum) in southern Italy, south of Naples, was a rich Greek colony and has the best preserved ancient temples anywhere in the Greek world. This one, built in the sixth century B.C. in the Doric style and known as the temple of Ceres (the Roman version of Demeter), was in fact dedicated to the goddess Athena and later used as a Christian church. For hundreds of years few people visited the site of Paestum because it was hidden by swamps and undergrowth, and this accounts for the remarkably good condition of the buildings today.

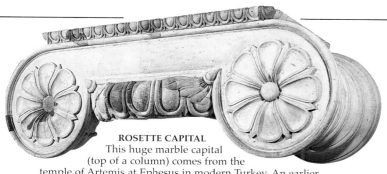

ROSETTE CAPITAL
This huge marble capital (top of a column) comes from the temple of Artemis at Ephesus in modern Turkey. An earlier temple on the same site was destroyed by fire in 356 B.C. on the same night that Alexander the Great (pp. 84–85) was born.

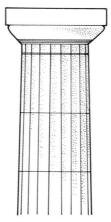
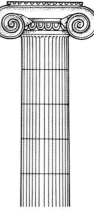
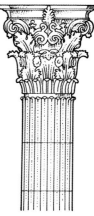

DORIC
The Doric style is sturdy, and its top (the capital) is plain. This style was used in mainland Greece and the colonies in southern Italy and Sicily.

IONIC
The Ionic style is thinner and more elegant. Its capital is decorated with a scroll-like design (a volute). This style was used in eastern Greece and the islands.

CORINTHIAN
The Corinthian style was seldom used in the Greek world, but often appeared in Roman temples. Its capital is elaborate and decorated with acanthus leaves.

LION'S MOUTH
Rain water was sometimes drained away from the roofs of temples through spouts in the form of lions' heads. This one comes from a temple of Athena at Priene, just south of Ephesus, in modern Turkey.

COLUMNS AND CAPITALS
Most Greek buildings had vertical columns and horizontal lintels (beams). This style of construction may have been inspired by earlier wooden buildings whose roofs were supported by tree trunks.

CORINTHIAN CAPITAL
This Corinthian capital once decorated a gracious colonnaded building in Asia Minor (modern Turkey). The face is a version of a female theatrical mask. The deeply carved leaves below copy those of the acanthus plant, a favorite design of Greek artists. The plant is easily identified by its spreading, leathery leaves.

PALMETTE ROOF TILE
The end of this roof tile is decorated with a palmette shape. It comes from a temple to Apollo at Bassae in southern Greece. This area was famous for its fighting men, and Apollo may have been worshiped here as a god of soldiers.

LOTUS LEAVES
This marble fragment is crisply carved with a frieze of lotus and palmette designs and other delicate moldings. It comes from the top part of the east wall of the temple of the Erechtheion on the Acropolis of Athens (pp. 58–59). The roof of the south porch of the building is supported by columns in the form of standing women with baskets on their heads. Pericles ordered the construction of the Erechtheion (which survives today on the site of older buildings) in the middle fifth century B.C. to beautify the city of Athens.

Women's world

Whorl

SPINDLE
Wool was spun into yarn with a spindle. This one is made of wood, but bronze and bone examples also exist. At one end is a weight, known as a spindle whorl. The spindle twirls around and spins the wool fiber into thread.

T HE LIVES OF WOMEN in ancient Greece were restricted. Women were very much under the control of their husbands, fathers, or brothers, and rarely took part in politics or any form of public life. Most women could not inherit property and were allowed very little money. A girl would marry very young, at the age of 13 or 14. Her husband, who was certain to be much older, was chosen for her by her father. The main purpose of marriage was to have a baby, preferably a boy, to carry on the male line. The status of a woman greatly increased when she had given birth to a boy (pp. 70–71). Some marriages seem to have been happy. A number of tombstones have survived that commemorate women who died in childbirth. There are tender inscriptions from the grieving husbands. It is possible that, although legally they had very little freedom, some women could make important decisions about family life. Their spinning and weaving work made an important contribution to the household.

Greek Woman by British artist Sir Lawrence Alma-Tadema (1836-1912)

HOMEMAKERS
Girls in Greece did not go to school (pp. 70–71). Instead, they stayed at home and were taught by their mothers how to spin and weave and look after the house. Some wealthier women were taught to read and write. On this vase a woman is reading from a papyrus scroll.

SPINNER
On this white-ground jug a woman is spinning with both a distaff and spindle. The distaff was a shaft of wood or metal with a spike at one end and a handle at the other.

WELL WOMEN
Few houses had their own private wells, and in Athens women and slave girls went to public fountains to fill their water pots. The water spout at this fountain is shaped like a lion's head. The women wait their turn, their water pots balanced on their heads. This was a good opportunity to meet with friends and chat.

This *epinetron* has a scene of spinning and weaving painted upon it in the black-figure technique

THIGH PROTECTOR
Spinning and weaving were regarded as suitable occupations for all Greek women, even those of noble families. In preparing the wool for spinning, a woman fitted a special instrument called an *epinetron* over her knee. She then rolled the wool across the surface and drew it out, producing thin skeins of wool.

SAPPHO
Sappho, a woman writer of the late seventh century B.C., lived on the island of Lesbos in the eastern Aegean. Women in this part of Greece seem to have had more freedom than the women of Athens, and Sappho's beautiful poems give us a glimpse of their lives and their feelings.

BEAUTY AID
Wealthy women owned many beauty aids. This bronze mirror has a stand in the form of a goddess, probably Aphrodite, holding a dove. Two little cupid figures fly on either side of her. This mirror would have been highly polished when new, so that its owner could see her reflection in it. Caskets, combs, and perfume bottles have also been found in large numbers.

The little lamps burning on the tables in front of the diners were probably used to keep dishes hot

ENTERTAINERS
Respectable women were expected to stay at home as much as possible, keeping house and supervising the slaves. Only women called *hetaerae* were allowed to attend the *symposia* (banquets), an important part of Greek social life. *Hetaerae* can be seen on vases, playing the pipes, dancing, and generally entertaining the male banqueters. Many *hetaerae* were foreigners or prisoners taken in wars.

69

Growing up in Greece

THE FUTURE OF A BABY rested entirely in the hands of its father. When a baby was born, the mother handed it to the father, who could decide whether or not to let it live. If the baby was a girl or was not strong, or if the family could not afford to keep it, the father might decide to abandon it. Then the baby would be left in the open air to die. Some abandoned babies were saved by other families and brought up as slaves. However, once a baby had been formally accepted by its family and named on the tenth day after its birth, he or she was treated kindly. Many toys have been found, and writers tell of games like blindman's buff. In Athens and most other Greek towns, boys went to school from about the age of seven. Girls did not go to school. At about the age of 12 or 13, children were considered to be young adults and would then dedicate their toys to the god Apollo and the goddess Artemis, as a sign that they had reached the end of childhood.

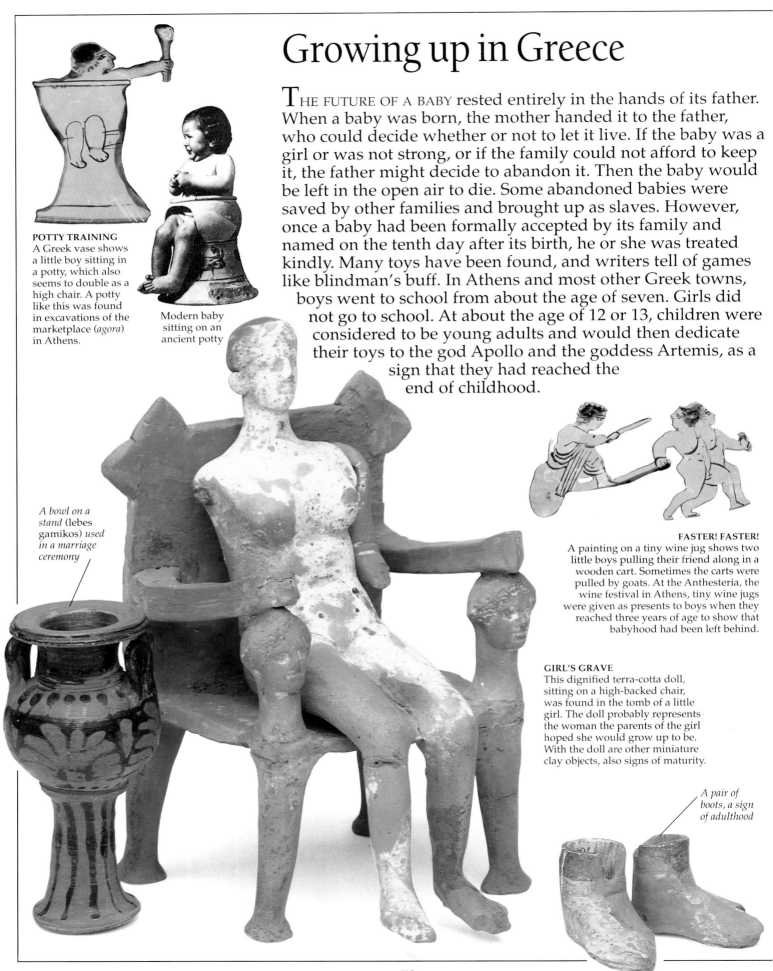

POTTY TRAINING
A Greek vase shows a little boy sitting in a potty, which also seems to double as a high chair. A potty like this was found in excavations of the marketplace (*agora*) in Athens.

Modern baby sitting on an ancient potty

A bowl on a stand (lebes gamikos) *used in a marriage ceremony*

FASTER! FASTER!
A painting on a tiny wine jug shows two little boys pulling their friend along in a wooden cart. Sometimes the carts were pulled by goats. At the Anthesteria, the wine festival in Athens, tiny wine jugs were given as presents to boys when they reached three years of age to show that babyhood had been left behind.

GIRL'S GRAVE
This dignified terra-cotta doll, sitting on a high-backed chair, was found in the tomb of a little girl. The doll probably represents the woman the parents of the girl hoped she would grow up to be. With the doll are other miniature clay objects, also signs of maturity.

A pair of boots, a sign of adulthood

Education

When boys went to school at seven, they learned reading, writing, and arithmetic from a teacher called a *grammatistes*. They learned music, including the playing of an instrument, from a teacher known as a *kitharistes*. They also had to memorize poetry and learn the art of debating. Older boys were taught by teachers called Sophists. Sophists traveled from town to town and often taught their students in the *gymnasia*, or training grounds. Girls did not go to school, but some girls from well-off families had private tutors who taught them to read and write. From their mothers they learned spinning, weaving, and how to run a home.

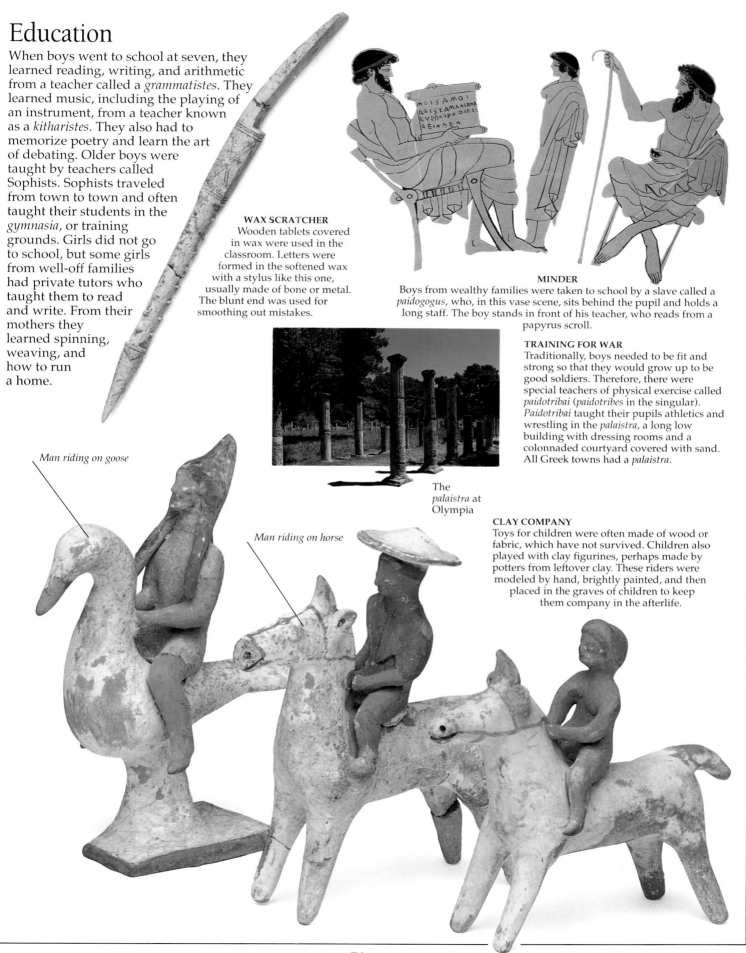

WAX SCRATCHER
Wooden tablets covered in wax were used in the classroom. Letters were formed in the softened wax with a stylus like this one, usually made of bone or metal. The blunt end was used for smoothing out mistakes.

MINDER
Boys from wealthy families were taken to school by a slave called a *paidogogus*, who, in this vase scene, sits behind the pupil and holds a long staff. The boy stands in front of his teacher, who reads from a papyrus scroll.

TRAINING FOR WAR
Traditionally, boys needed to be fit and strong so that they would grow up to be good soldiers. Therefore, there were special teachers of physical exercise called *paidotribai* (*paidotribes* in the singular). *Paidotribai* taught their pupils athletics and wrestling in the *palaistra*, a long low building with dressing rooms and a colonnaded courtyard covered with sand. All Greek towns had a *palaistra*.

The *palaistra* at Olympia

Man riding on goose

Man riding on horse

CLAY COMPANY
Toys for children were often made of wood or fabric, which have not survived. Children also played with clay figurines, perhaps made by potters from leftover clay. These riders were modeled by hand, brightly painted, and then placed in the graves of children to keep them company in the afterlife.

71

A day out

GREEK THEATERS ARE AMONG the most spectacular buildings that survive from ancient times. In cities like Athens or at sacred sites like Delphi and Epidaurus, people flocked to see dramas in honor of the gods. In Athens, performances for the wine god Dionysus developed into what are now known as plays. From the middle of the sixth century B.C., these plays were organized as competitions and were put on during the spring festival of Dionysus. By the fifth century B.C., both tragedies and comedies were performed and many have survived to the present time. Audiences in Athens spent days watching the plays, seated in the theater of Dionysus on the slope of the Acropolis. All of the actors were men, taking the female parts as well, and no more than three main actors could speak to each other at one time. A larger group of actors, the chorus, commented on the play's action and addressed the audience more directly. Music accompanied the plays, which were acted out on a flat circular area called the orchestra. Women were probably not allowed to go to the theater at all.

TIRED OUT
This small terra-cotta figure shows a comic actor dressed as an old woman. He wears a mask with a wrinkled face and crinkly hair that he has pushed back on his head, as he rests wearily on a seat.

EURIPIDES
The expression on this sculpture reflects the serious subjects dealt with by the Athenian playwright Euripides. Some of his plays were about the horrors of war, which upset the Athenians because they hinted at Athens' savage treatment of her enemies.

BIRD'S EYE VIEW
From high up in the back row at Epidaurus you can get a clear view of the performance. Here, a temporary set has been built for the modern production of a play.

EPIDAURUS
This ground-level view of the 14,000-seat theater at Epidaurus gives an idea of what it is like to be an actor going into the performing area. The carefully curved auditorium (*theatron*, or viewing theater) is a huge semicircular bowl cut into the surface of the hillside. Its shape is not just designed for excellent viewing; sound, too, is caught and amplified, and actors speaking in the orchestra can be heard in the back row.

SOPHOCLES

Portraits of famous playwrights were produced some time after their death, so they were not true likenesses. But these sculptures honored the memory of great writers like the playwright Sophocles. This print decorates a 19th-century text of the plays. Sophocles' plays about royal or legendary families and their tragic lives, like those of King Oedipus or Electra, daughter of Agamemnon, still grip audiences today.

GREEK DRAMA ALIVE AND WELL

A group of actors from Britain's Royal National Theatre perform three plays called *The Oresteia*, by the Athenian playwright Aeschylus. They tell of the death of Agamemnon after the Trojan War and how his son Orestes avenged him.

The elaborate hat is a sign that this bearded man's wealth was not acquired honestly

The muse holds a mask portraying a young woman, one of the characters in a Greek comedy from the fourth century B.C.

SOUVENIR STATUETTES

Statuettes in terra cotta, originally painted in bright colors, are perhaps souvenirs of theater visits. Sets of the entire casts of plays have been found in graves. The graceful female figure is probably a muse, one of the nine guardians of the arts in Greek mythology. The terra cotta of the bearded actor represents a sinister figure from later Greek comedy, who lived off the earnings of *hetaerae*.

Wisdom and beauty

For the Greeks, philosophy, or the "love of wisdom," involved not just the way people lived, but a great deal of science as well. Early thinkers were concerned with ideas about the physical world. Heraclitus developed a theory involving atoms, and Pythagoras came up with a geometrical theory as part of his view that the world was based on mathematical patterns. He and his fellow thinkers, both men and women, also believed that souls could be reincarnated – reborn in other bodies – and some even thought that beans might contain the souls of old friends and therefore shouldn't be eaten. Philosophy and the arts were part of religion too. Religious hymns celebrated the meaning of life and explained the origin of the gods. The Greeks made handsome objects both as offerings to the gods and also for their own pleasure and use. Music, sculpture, painting, pottery, and dance all thrived in ancient Greece.

ROYAL PUPIL
Greek philosophers were at the center of Greek life. Here, the philosopher Aristotle is tutoring the young prince Alexander of Macedon (pp. 84–85).

PIPED MUSIC
This pipe from Athens, made out of sycamore wood, is one of a pair; Greeks played sets of double pipes. There was originally a reed in the mouthpiece, so the pipes would have sounded a bit like a modern oboe.

VASE PAINTER
Vase painting is considered to be one of the minor arts, but the work of the potter and painter Exekias was of a very high standard. This exquisitely painted drinking cup shows the god Dionysos reclining in a boat, with his special plant, the vine, twining around the mast. The god, like the vine, was believed to have come from the East. The dolphins may be the pirates who tried to capture him, now turned into sea creatures.

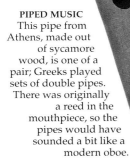

ANIMAL AMPLIFIER
The European tortoise was once plentiful in Greece, and its empty shell made an excellent soundbox for a stringed instrument called the lyre. Its strings, which were plucked with a plectrum (pick), could be tightened to produce a range of notes.

Pythagoras holding the cosmos

THE KEY TO THE COSMOS
Pythagoras (c.580–500 B.C.), originally from the island of Samos, was the leading light of a group of religious thinkers in southern Italy. They believed that the key to the world (cosmos) lay in numbers and mathematical relationships.

SEEING EYE TO EYE

The eye was an important symbol in ancient Greece. It gave life and power to objects. Eyes were painted on statues; eyes on the front of warships magically guided them. This eye cup of the sixth century B.C. blends the elements of a face with the patterns found on many wine-cups. The eyebrows are echoed by long strands of ivy, a plant associated with Dionysus. A pair of his satyr friends are escaping around the sides of the cup. The eyes themselves have perfectly formed circles incised with a sharp-pointed tool.

Cup has no flat base and was probably passed around from hand to hand

DEATH BY HEMLOCK

Socrates' teachings were so astonishing, even for the fairly broad-minded Athenians, that some people became suspicious of him. He was accused of corrupting the minds of the young and showing disrespect for the gods. He was imprisoned, then made to take his own life by drinking a poison, hemlock.

FOUNDING FATHERS

Side by side, with proud gestures, philosophers Aristotle (384–322 B.C.) and Plato (427–347 B.C.) are outlined against the sky, each holding one of their major books. The Italian artist Raphael (1483–1520) has placed them in the very center of his fresco, painted on the wall of a great room in the Vatican in the early 16th century.

WORD OF MOUTH

Although Socrates (469–399 B.C.) is one of the most famous of the ancient Greek philosophers, he produced no philosophical writings. He explored philosophy by discussing it intently, often pretending to be ignorant of a subject in order to allow his opponents to unintentionally destroy their destroy their own argument. Socrates has a bare chest in this marble statuette; philosophers were often shown dressed in this way.

PLATO AND PUPILS

The leading philosophers attracted groups of pupils, and much teaching was done in discussion groups. Plato set up a school for philosophers in Athens, his native city, in a pleasant garden called the Academy. Plato wrote up many ideas of Socrates in the form of "dialogues" or discussions between pupils and teachers.

Science and medicine

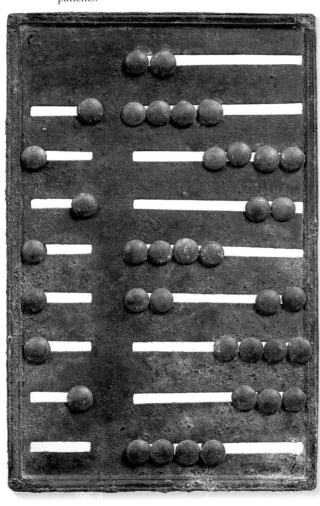

THE GREEKS WERE INTERESTED in science and, influenced by Egyptian and Babylonian scholars, made advances in biology, mathematics, astrology, and geography. In the third century B.C., the astronomer, Aristarchus, already understood that the earth revolved around the sun, and another astronomer, Anaxagoras (500–428 B.C.), discovered that the moon reflected sunlight. The most advanced scientific work took place in Hellenistic times (pp. 84–85). An important area of Greek science was medicine. The Greeks believed that illness was a punishment sent by the gods to whom they prayed for a cure. Sanctuaries of the god Asclepius (the god of medicine) were found all over the Greek world. The most famous one was at Epidaurus. Many sick people came there and spent the night in the temple. They believed that Asclepius appeared to them in "dreams" to prescribe treatments such as herbal remedies, diets, and exercises. The next day, the priests would carry out the treatment and many people went away cured. The Greeks developed sophisticated medical treatments for all kinds of diseases. These treatments, based on practical research, grew out of the Asclepiad cult and were practised by Hippocrates (460–377 B.C.) who is often described as the founder of modern medicine.

IT ALL ADDS UP
This engraving from a philosophy book of the 1400s shows the Roman philosopher Boethius (A.D. 480–524) doing mathematical calculations, and the Greek mathematician Pythagoras (pp. 74–75) working at an abacus. The woman in the center is probably a muse of learning.

TEMPLE OF ASCLEPIUS
In this engraving, people can be seen approaching a statue of the god Asclepius. He is sitting on a throne and holding his staff which has a serpent twisted round it. A real snake, regarded as sacred and kept in all temples to Asclepius, can be seen slithering along the plinth.

ABACUS
The Greeks used a counting frame called an abacus for mathematical calculations. It had beads threaded in lines on wires. Some lines had beads which counted as 1, others had the value of 10 and others, 100. By moving the beads around, complicated multiplication and division could be achieved.

TEMPLE VISIT
In this painting by the 19th-century artist John William Waterhouse (1849–1917) a child has been brought by his mother to the temple of Asclepius. Priests stand around waiting to interpret the god's wishes.

THANKS

Patients who had been cured by Asclepius often left a model of the part of their body affected by illness, as an offering of thanks to the god for curing them. This marble relief of a leg has an inscription to Asclepius carved upon it and was dedicated by a worshipper called Tyche.

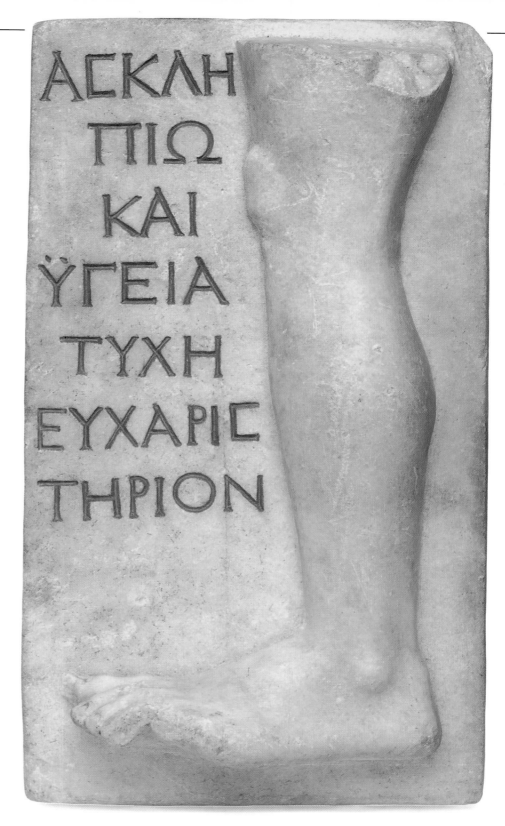

HIPPOCRATES

The famous physician, Hippocrates, was born on the island of Kos. He wrote 53 scientific books on medical topics, now known as the *Corpus*. He taught that the human body was a single organism and each part could only be understood in the context of the whole. Modern doctors still take the Hippocratic Oath which is the basis of medical ethics.

MODERN MODELS

The practice of leaving a model of the affected part of the body as a thanks offering, still continues in churches in some countries today. These modern examples are from Athens.

TOKENS

These modern silver tokens are also thanks for cures. The animals indicate that people believed that they too could be cured with the help of offerings.

Crafts, travel, and trade

STONE CARVERS, METAL WORKERS, jewelers, shoemakers, and many other craftspeople flourished in the cities of Greece. Their workshops were usually in the center of town around the *agora*, or marketplace. People would come to buy their products, and farmers from the countryside would sell vegetables, fruit, and cheese. There were also weights-and-measures officials, money-changers, acrobats, dancers, and slaves standing on platforms waiting to be sold. Most ordinary people did not travel far from home (except to war), because there were few good roads. The faithful donkey was the most reliable form of transport for shorter journeys. If a Greek wanted to travel a long distance, he would usually go by boat around the coast, thereby avoiding the mountains that cover much of the country. There was a great deal of trade between the city-states and the Greek colonies, as well as with other Mediterranean countries. Oil, wine, pottery, and metal work were the main exports.

FISHY BUSINESS
Fishing provides a livelihood for many Greeks today, just as it did in ancient times. A modern fisherman on the island of Mykonos is mending his nets.

TEMPLE TREASURE
This clay jug with coins was found in the foundations of the temple of Artemis at Ephesus. The coins, made of electrum, probably date from 650–625 B.C. This was soon after coinage was introduced into Greece from Lydia in Asia Minor (roughly, modern Turkey), where coins were invented.

Coin showing the infant Herakles strangling snakes

THREE COINS
As a symbol of independence, each city-state issued its own coins, which were at first made of electrum (an alloy of gold and silver) and later solely of silver or occasionally gold. They were often beautifully decorated with the symbols of Greek deities, and many modern coins have been modeled on them.

Coin showing Cyrus, the king of Persia

A tortoise coin from the island of Aegina

INTO AFRICA
This pot in the form of the head of an African is evidence of the widespread trading contacts of the Greeks. They were not, however, very adventurous sailors, preferring to keep the coast in sight when on long voyages.

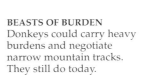

BEASTS OF BURDEN
Donkeys could carry heavy burdens and negotiate narrow mountain tracks. They still do today.

COBBLER
This cobbler is depicted at the bottom of a red figure cup. He is bending over strips of leather that he is cutting and shaping. Boots, sandals, and tools hang from the wall above him. This scene would have become visible to the drinker when he had drained his cup.

AT THE LOOM
Upright looms, just like this one in use today, were used by women in Classical times to make woolen clothing, drapes, and furniture fabrics. Weaving was regarded as a noble as well as a necessary task.

BLACKSMITH
This painting on a jug shows a blacksmith at work. His furnace is a brick-built shaft fueled with charcoal. Bellows would have been used to fan the flames. The metal, which was placed inside the shaft, trickled down to form a lump at the bottom, which the blacksmith can here be seen removing with a pair of tongs.

POTTER
The Greeks are famous for their beautiful pottery. Every town had its potters' quarter where pots were made and sold. On this wine cup, a potter sits at his wheel, the speed of which he controls with his knee. Above him on a shelf are some of his pots, and below him (now slightly damaged) sits a pet dog who is watching his master at work.

DEEP-SEA FISHING
A great variety of fish were available in the deeper waters. Wooden vessels, like this modern one, were used for such fishing expeditions. Eel and salted fish were favorite Greek delicacies.

The Greek games

CHAMPIONS
This fourth-century B.C. bronze statue of a boy jockey and his victorious horse shows the difficulties of racing in ancient Greece. Jockeys, who were usually paid servants of the horse's owner, rode without stirrups.

THE GREEKS BELIEVED IN THE VALUE of sports as training for warfare and as a way of honoring the gods. There were many local sporting competitions, and four big athletic festivals that attracted men from all over the Greek world. Of these, the most important was the Olympic Games, held at Olympia every four years in honor of Zeus. Success in the Games brought honor to the athlete's family and to his hometown, and some successful athletes acquired almost mythical status. Wars were sometimes suspended to allow people to travel in safety to and from Olympia. Many beautiful temples and other buildings that provided facilities for athletes and spectators have been excavated there. The Games went on into Roman times, coming to an end late in the fourth century. In Athens, there were also the Panathenaic Games, which were held every four years in honor of Athena as part of her religious festival; they were an important public holiday. Discipline in sports was strict, and rule breakers were punished severely.

TRAINING TIME
Wrestling, although popular, was regarded as one of the most dangerous of Greek sports. Tripping your opponent was permitted, but biting or gouging out his eyes was strictly forbidden. The man on the left of this statue base is in a racing start position, and the man on the right is testing his javelin.

PRIZE POTS
This boxing scene (336 B.C.) was painted on a special kind of olive oil pot given as a prize to victorious athletes at the festival of Athena in Athens. Known as Panathenaic vases, they always had a painting of Athena on one side and a painting of the event on the other. Here, two boxers with rippling muscles are fighting each other. Instead of boxing gloves, they wear leather thongs wrapped around their fists.

THE DELPHI STADIUM
The stadium at Delphi is in the highest part of the ancient city. The stone starting grooves on the track survive, as well as many of the seats, particularly those cut into the mountain side. The stadium could hold 7,000 spectators.

THE OLYMPIC SPIRIT
The spirit of the Olympic Games has greatly inspired artists. This 19th-century German picture depicts naked athletes exercising against a background of classical columns.

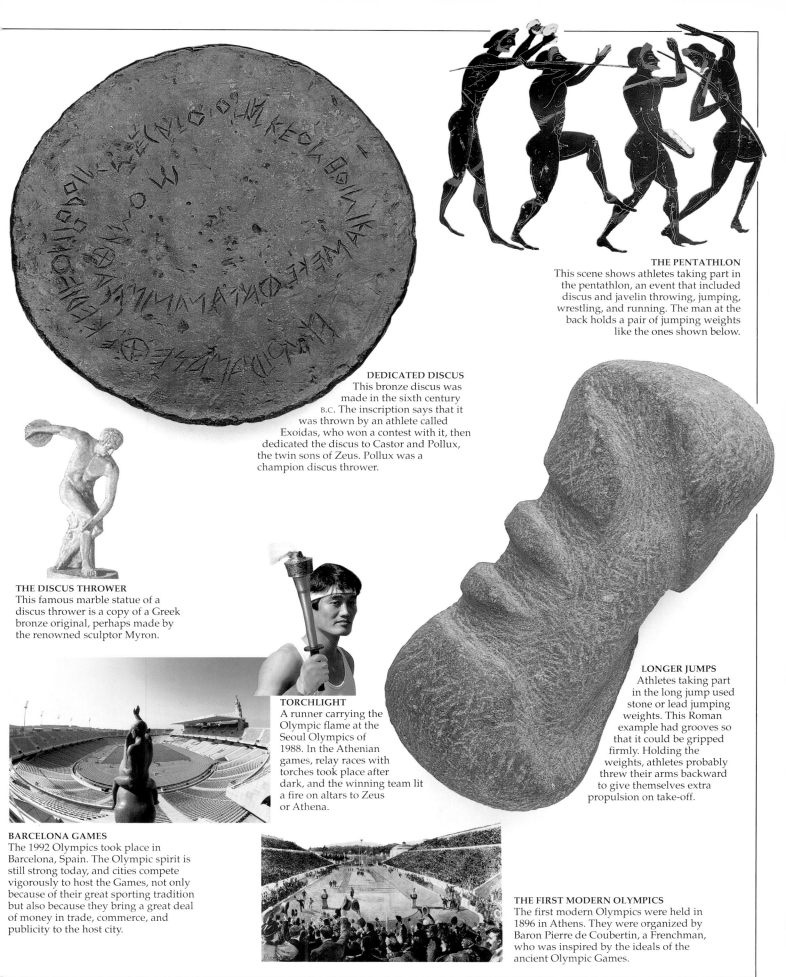

THE PENTATHLON
This scene shows athletes taking part in the pentathlon, an event that included discus and javelin throwing, jumping, wrestling, and running. The man at the back holds a pair of jumping weights like the ones shown below.

DEDICATED DISCUS
This bronze discus was made in the sixth century B.C. The inscription says that it was thrown by an athlete called Exoidas, who won a contest with it, then dedicated the discus to Castor and Pollux, the twin sons of Zeus. Pollux was a champion discus thrower.

THE DISCUS THROWER
This famous marble statue of a discus thrower is a copy of a Greek bronze original, perhaps made by the renowned sculptor Myron.

TORCHLIGHT
A runner carrying the Olympic flame at the Seoul Olympics of 1988. In the Athenian games, relay races with torches took place after dark, and the winning team lit a fire on altars to Zeus or Athena.

LONGER JUMPS
Athletes taking part in the long jump used stone or lead jumping weights. This Roman example had grooves so that it could be gripped firmly. Holding the weights, athletes probably threw their arms backward to give themselves extra propulsion on take-off.

BARCELONA GAMES
The 1992 Olympics took place in Barcelona, Spain. The Olympic spirit is still strong today, and cities compete vigorously to host the Games, not only because of their great sporting tradition but also because they bring a great deal of money in trade, commerce, and publicity to the host city.

THE FIRST MODERN OLYMPICS
The first modern Olympics were held in 1896 in Athens. They were organized by Baron Pierre de Coubertin, a Frenchman, who was inspired by the ideals of the ancient Olympic Games.

Warfare

Helmet with nose protection

Body armor

SHIELDED
This Greek vase painting shows how the soldier wore his shield, passing his arm under an iron bar and gripping a leather strap at the rim.

WARFARE WAS a normal part of Greek life, and the city-states frequently fought one another. Many Greek men, therefore, had to join an army, and from the earliest times had to pay for their own armor and equipment. In Athens, boys trained as soldiers between age 18 and 20, after which they could be called up for military service. In Sparta training began much earlier (pp. 54–55). Athenian soldiers were led by ten commanders called *strategoi*. The infantry (foot soldiers) were the backbone of the Greek armies; they fought in close formations called phalanxes. Poorer soldiers served in auxiliary units as archers and stoneslingers. When laying siege to cities, the armies of Hellenistic Greece used catapults, flame throwers, battering rams, and cauldrons of burning coals and sulfur. Athens controlled its empire by means of oar-powered warships, or triremes. At the height of its power, it had about 300 triremes.

BATTLE OF SALAMIS
The famous sea battle of Salamis was a turning point in the Persian wars. It took place just off the coast of Athens in 480 B.C. and was a triumphant victory for the Greeks over the Persian fleet. As a result of this battle, the Persian king Xerxes and much of his army went back to Asia, abandoning the invasion of Greece.

SPEEDY BEASTS
Greek chariots were often decorated with animals associated with speed. These bronze horses were once attached to a fast chariot.

NAKED BRAVERY
In this painted scene from a vase, a warrior is holding a metal cuirass (body armor). He also has a long spear and a shield. In Greek art nakedness is a symbol of heroic bravery.

HOPLITE
Greek soldiers were called hoplites, from the word *hoplon*, meaning shield. Only men from wealthy families could be hoplites, because only they could afford expensive armor and weapons.

Greaves

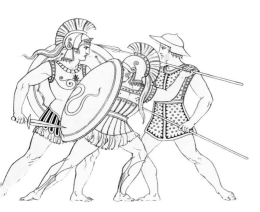

FOOT COMBAT
A painted vase shows two Greek combatants separated by a messenger.

HELMETS
Helmets protected the head from every sort of slash and from blows and knocks. They varied in shape, and some had crests made of horsehair to make the wearer appear more impressive and frightening.

Attic helmet has no nose guard

Corinthian helmet with long nosepiece and cheek guards

BREASTPLATE
The cuirass (breastplate or body armor) was usually made of bronze. It protected all the upper body parts. Cuirasses were made to measure, each man being specially fitted. More expensive cuirasses had ridges, roughly aligned to the body muscles, which were meant to deflect blows. The cuirass was made of two plates joined at the sides by leather straps. The side areas, therefore, were the most vulnerable parts of the body.

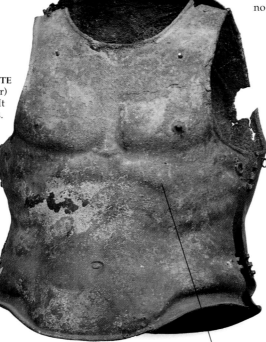

GREAVES
Hoplites wore bronze leg guards called greaves (below) to protect the lower part of their legs in battle. Some of these greaves may have originally been fixed onto large statues of heroic warriors in southern Italy.

Sculpted ridges roughly aligning with chest muscles

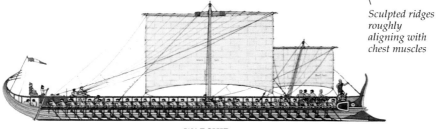

WARSHIP
The fastest Greek ship was called a trireme; 170 oarsmen were needed to row it. They sat in three levels, one above the other, on either side of the boat. At the prow was a pointed ram strengthened with metal, which could sink enemy ships. There was often an eye painted on the prow (pp. 74–75). This illustration shows two sails, but warships may have had only one, probably made of linen and lowered when the ship was engaged in battle.

The long spear was the main weapon of the Greek infantry

CHAMPION FIGHT
This red-figure vase shows a fight between two heroes of the Trojan War, Achilles and Hector (pp. 52–53). The vase painter has clearly painted the blood flowing from the wound just above Hector's knee. Both heroes are wearing the helmets and armor worn by soldiers of the 5th century B.C.

Alexander and the Hellenistic age

IN THE FOURTH CENTURY B.C., a strong king called Philip II turned Macedonia, in the north, into the most powerful state in Greece. After his assassination in 336 B.C., his 20-year-old son Alexander, a military genius, took over the reins of power. Not content with ruling Greece, he invaded Persian territory in 334 B.C. and then pressed on through Asia Minor, then south and east to Egypt, Afghanistan, and India. He established new Greek cities, such as Alexandria in Egypt, and thus spread Greek culture over a vast area. Alexander, called the Great, intended to create a huge empire, incorporating most of the then known world. His death of a fever in 323 B.C. ended this ambition, and his vast empire was divided among his quarreling generals. The period from the death of Alexander until about 30 B.C. is known as the Hellenistic Age, from the word "Hellene," meaning Greek. The Hellenistic kingdoms preserved many aspects of Greek life but were eventually overcome by the rising power of Rome.

EXCAVATION AT EPHESUS
Ephesus was a teeming city on the coast of Asia Minor where Greeks and people of many other nationalities lived together. The city and its famous sanctuary, dedicated to the goddess Artemis, thrived in the Hellenistic period and throughout the Roman era.

ONE MAN AND HIS DOG
This charming ring from the Hellenistic period is decorated with a scene of a shepherd with his dog and his crook.

APHRODITE
Terra-cotta figurines of Aphrodite, goddess of love and beauty, were popular in Hellenistic times. She is nearly always shown without any clothes, sometimes tying a ribbon in her hair, sometimes bending down to fasten her sandal.

Ruins at Pergamum

TOWN PLANNING
Pergamum, a Hellenistic city in Asia Minor, was the power base of the wealthy Attalid dynasty. The ruins of temples and other opulent civic buildings can still be seen on the terraces cut into the steep mountain site. The people of Pergamum must have enjoyed spectacular views over the surrounding countryside.

Ruins at Pergamum

EROS DIADEM
Alexander's troops captured a great deal of Persian gold, and gold jewelry became very fashionable in aristocratic circles. Elaborate diadems, closely resembling crowns, have been found. Fixed at the front of this spectacular diadem is a tiny figure of Eros, the personification of love, holding a jug.

ALEXANDER'S EMPIRE

Alexander did not just want to build an empire, he also wanted it to last. To stop rebellion and invasion by conquered peoples, he founded many colonies populated by his own former soldiers who followed the Greek way of life. On the whole he treated the conquered peoples with respect and encouraged his men to marry Eastern women. His conquests came to an end in India because his men refused to fight any farther.

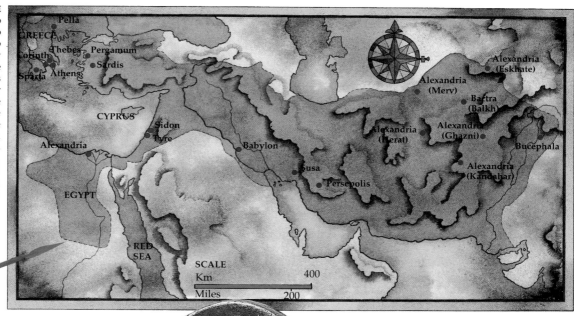

Richard Burton in the 1956 film
Alexander the Great

TRUNK CHARGER

This coin shows Alexander on horseback attacking two Indian warriors mounted on an elephant. It is thought to have been issued in Babylon in 323 B.C.

WALL OF FIRE

In 327 B.C., Alexander crossed the Himalayan Mountains intending to conquer India. But a terrible battle forced him to turn back to Babylon. Alexander's fame lived on in legend. This Indian painting, painted over 1,000 years after his time, shows him building a defensive wall of fire.

THE DEFEAT OF DARIUS

Alexander finally defeated the Persian king Darius III in 331 B.C. in a long and bloody battle at Gaugamela in Mesopotamia (southwest Asia). Darius fled, and afterward Alexander called himself King of Asia. In this etching, he can be seen on horseback, fighting fearlessly.

FAMILY OF DARIUS

In this painting by the Italian artist Paolo Veronese (1528–1588), Alexander is shown receiving the submission of the family of his defeated enemy Darius. Notice that the artist has portrayed everyone in 16th-century clothes.

City-state to superpower

ACCORDING TO LEGEND, Rome was founded in 753 B.C. by the brothers Romulus and Remus, sons of the war god Mars. It was built on seven hills beside the Tiber River, on the border of Etruria. Early Rome was ruled by kings until 509 B.C., when the nobles drove out the wicked Etruscan king Tarquin the Proud. Rome became a republic, ruled by two consuls elected from the senate each year (p. 94). She overpowered her neighbors in Italy, and learned about Greek civilization from Greek city-states in the south. By 260 B.C. Rome had become a major force. A clash with the trading empire of Carthage in North Africa led to a century of terrible wars. Carthage was finally crushed in 146 B.C., leaving Rome as the greatest power in the Mediterranean.

The Etruscans

The Etruscan people lived in northern Italian city-states and were very influenced by Greece. They were great traders, architects, and engineers, and in turn influenced early Rome, especially its religion.

ETRUSCAN DESIGN
A three-horse chariot running over a fallen man is the design for this Etruscan toilet box leg. The Etruscans may have given Rome the idea of chariot racing (p. 114) and gladiator fights in the arena (p. 110).

REALISTIC ART
Part of a suit of armor, this shoulder guard shows a Greek grappling with one of the legendary Amazons (female warriors). The Romans admired and copied the very realistic figures of Greek art.

RIVER GOD
This little painted face of fired clay shows that the Greeks were skilled potters.

The Greeks

The Greeks had colonized the coasts of Sicily and southern Italy, and the fertile land had made many of the new cities wealthy, with splendid temples and richly furnished houses. These Greek colonies eventually came under Roman control, but brought with them their art, literature, and learning.

GODDESS OF LOVE
This silver plaque shows Aphrodite, the goddess of love. The Romans saw their goddess Venus like this.

AN ARMY OF ELEPHANTS

The growing power of Rome faced its stiffest test in 218 B.C. when the determined Carthaginian general Hannibal marched from Spain to Italy over the Alps, complete with war elephants, seen here in a 19th-century print. Hannibal smashed the legions sent against him, but Rome refused to admit defeat. He fought on in Italy for years while the Romans grimly held on, raising army after army, attacking Hannibal's bases in Spain and even landing in Africa. Finally the Carthaginians withdrew. Rome had won new lands, but the cost was terrible.

VICTORY SYMBOL

The Romans thought of the spirit of military victory as a goddess. The bronze statuette on the right shows her as an angel-like figure.

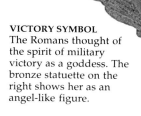

Victory statuette holds a crown of laurel leaves

Rome expands

The clash with Carthage left Rome with her first overseas provinces, and wars with other powerful states to the east soon followed. The generals who won these conflicts brought vast wealth to Rome, but also used their soldiers to fight for personal power in Italy. Civil wars raged across the Roman world.

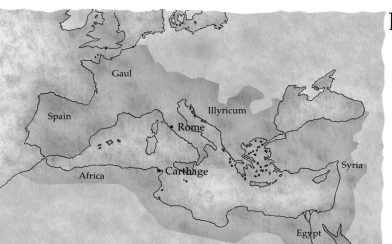

THE SHADOW OF ROME

The Roman Empire was divided up into different provinces. Most of the Mediterranean had fallen to Rome by 50 B.C. A few more provinces were added over the next 150 years, including Britain, and the Empire was at its height by the second century A.D.

DEATH TO A DICTATOR

The most famous warring general of the late republic, Julius Caesar defeated all his rivals and eventually ruled Rome as a permanent dictator. He was too much like a king for the proud Roman senators' (p. 94).

A SHIP OF WAR

The Romans learned from Carthage how to fight at sea. The clay plaque above shows a war galley, propelled by oars, with a ram at the front to sink other vessels. On the deck stand soldiers, ready to board and capture enemy ships in battle. In peacetime the fleet kept the sea lanes free of pirates.

The emperors

ROME WAS NOT ALWAYS RULED by emperors. For hundreds of years there was a republic (p. 86). But the republic collapsed in the chaos of civil wars both before and after Julius Caesar's death, when various generals fought for sole power. Order was finally restored when Julius Caesar's adopted son, Octavian (later called Augustus), was left as the only survivor of the warlords. A brilliant politician, he reformed the state and restored the Roman world to peace. He was in fact the sole ruler, with the power of the army to back him up, but he knew that Romans hated the idea of kingship. His clever solution was to proclaim the restoration of the old republic, with himself simply as first citizen. But the "new republic" was just for show; Augustus became, in fact, the first emperor, and when he died in A.D. 14, he passed the new throne to his adopted son Tiberius. Rome was to be ruled by emperors for the next 400 years.

Caligula went mad and was murdered: reigned A.D. 37-41

Claudius conquered Britain: reigned A.D. 41-54

Nero was the last of Augustus's family: reigned A.D. 54-68

HEADS AND TALES
In a world without newspapers, radio or television, coins were a good way to advertise to people the image of the emperor and his deeds. These are coins of Tiberius's successors.

A ROMAN TRIUMPH
When the emperor won a great victory, he would be granted a "triumph," the right to lead his soldiers through Rome with their prisoners and booty, while the people cheered. A slave stood behind him, holding a golden crown over his head. Captured enemy leaders would be strangled during the ceremonies.

MAD EMPEROR
Some Roman emperors went mad with power. Nero is the best known of these. Many blamed him for starting the great fire of Rome in A.D. 64, so that he could build himself a new capital on its ruins. He finally killed himself.

EMPEROR'S WEAPON
With its sword, this spectacular scabbard, decorated with gold and silver, was probably given to an officer by the emperor Tiberius himself. It was found in the Rhine River, Germany.

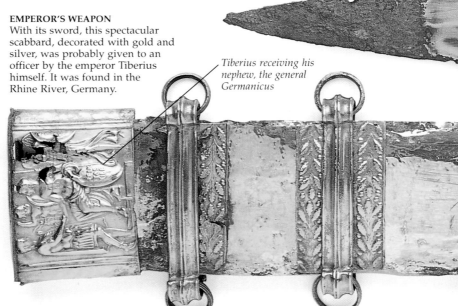

Tiberius receiving his nephew, the general Germanicus

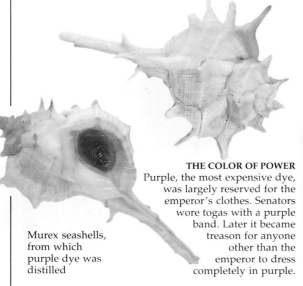

THE COLOR OF POWER
Purple, the most expensive dye, was largely reserved for the emperor's clothes. Senators wore togas with a purple band. Later it became treason for anyone other than the emperor to dress completely in purple.

Murex seashells, from which purple dye was distilled

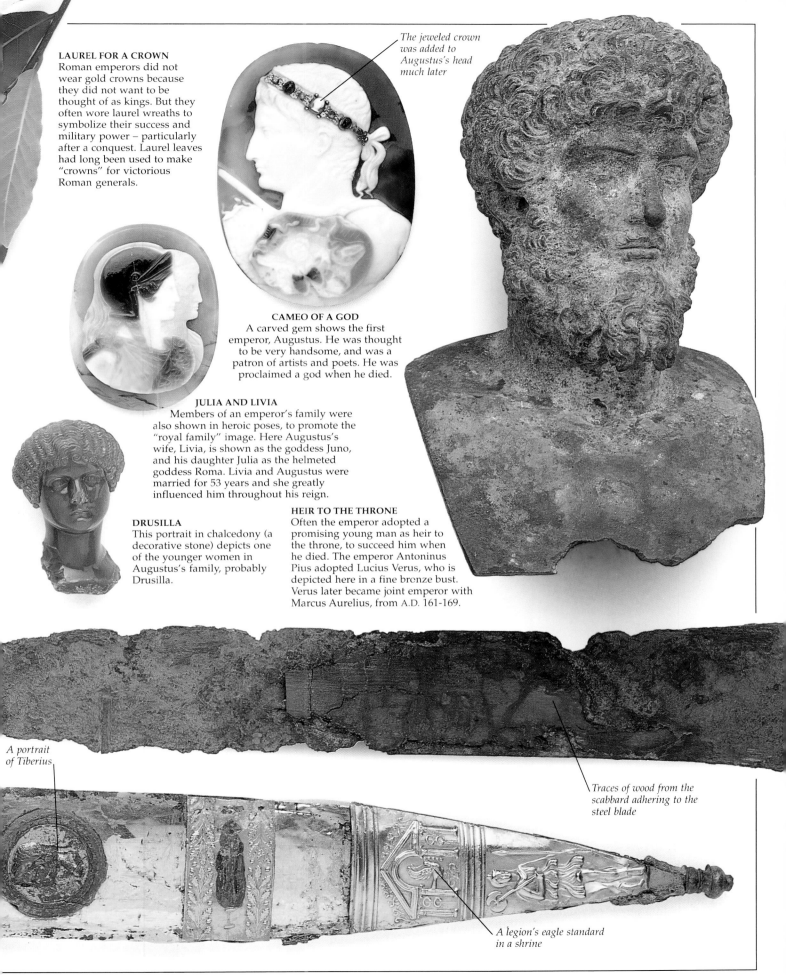

LAUREL FOR A CROWN
Roman emperors did not wear gold crowns because they did not want to be thought of as kings. But they often wore laurel wreaths to symbolize their success and military power – particularly after a conquest. Laurel leaves had long been used to make "crowns" for victorious Roman generals.

The jeweled crown was added to Augustus's head much later

CAMEO OF A GOD
A carved gem shows the first emperor, Augustus. He was thought to be very handsome, and was a patron of artists and poets. He was proclaimed a god when he died.

JULIA AND LIVIA
Members of an emperor's family were also shown in heroic poses, to promote the "royal family" image. Here Augustus's wife, Livia, is shown as the goddess Juno, and his daughter Julia as the helmeted goddess Roma. Livia and Augustus were married for 53 years and she greatly influenced him throughout his reign.

DRUSILLA
This portrait in chalcedony (a decorative stone) depicts one of the younger women in Augustus's family, probably Drusilla.

HEIR TO THE THRONE
Often the emperor adopted a promising young man as heir to the throne, to succeed him when he died. The emperor Antoninus Pius adopted Lucius Verus, who is depicted here in a fine bronze bust. Verus later became joint emperor with Marcus Aurelius, from A.D. 161-169.

A portrait of Tiberius

Traces of wood from the scabbard adhering to the steel blade

A legion's eagle standard in a shrine

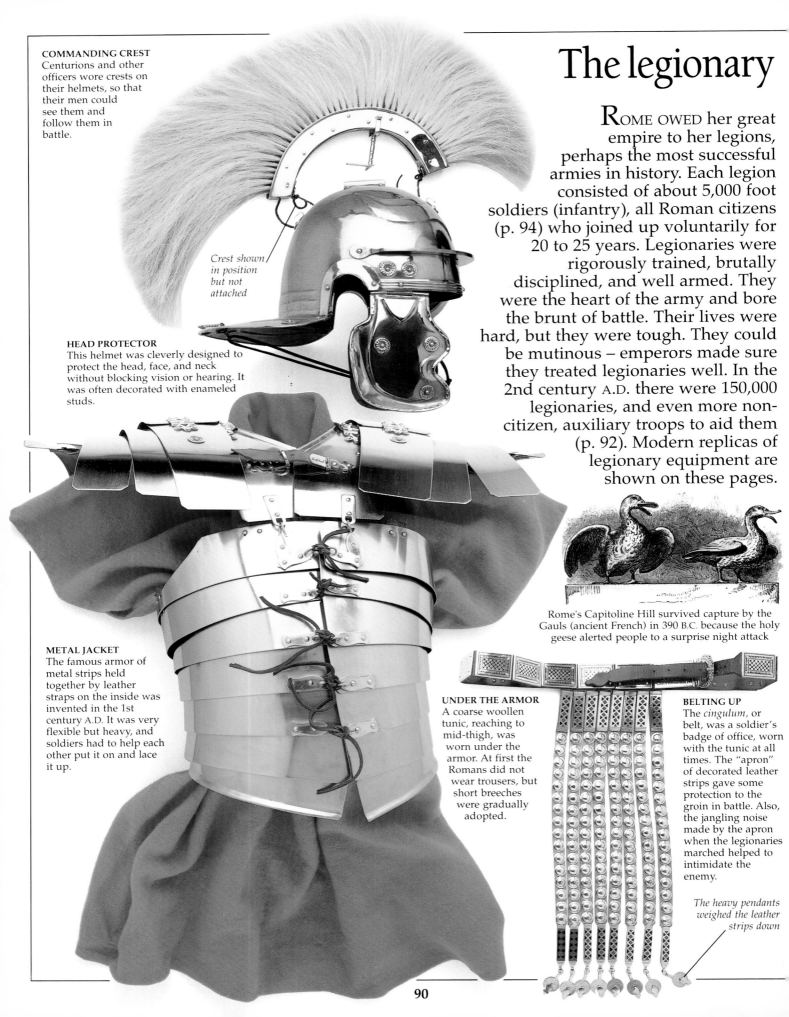

The legionary

COMMANDING CREST
Centurions and other officers wore crests on their helmets, so that their men could see them and follow them in battle.

Crest shown in position but not attached

HEAD PROTECTOR
This helmet was cleverly designed to protect the head, face, and neck without blocking vision or hearing. It was often decorated with enameled studs.

METAL JACKET
The famous armor of metal strips held together by leather straps on the inside was invented in the 1st century A.D. It was very flexible but heavy, and soldiers had to help each other put it on and lace it up.

ROME OWED her great empire to her legions, perhaps the most successful armies in history. Each legion consisted of about 5,000 foot soldiers (infantry), all Roman citizens (p. 94) who joined up voluntarily for 20 to 25 years. Legionaries were rigorously trained, brutally disciplined, and well armed. They were the heart of the army and bore the brunt of battle. Their lives were hard, but they were tough. They could be mutinous – emperors made sure they treated legionaries well. In the 2nd century A.D. there were 150,000 legionaries, and even more non-citizen, auxiliary troops to aid them (p. 92). Modern replicas of legionary equipment are shown on these pages.

Rome's Capitoline Hill survived capture by the Gauls (ancient French) in 390 B.C. because the holy geese alerted people to a surprise night attack

UNDER THE ARMOR
A coarse woollen tunic, reaching to mid-thigh, was worn under the armor. At first the Romans did not wear trousers, but short breeches were gradually adopted.

BELTING UP
The *cingulum*, or belt, was a soldier's badge of office, worn with the tunic at all times. The "apron" of decorated leather strips gave some protection to the groin in battle. Also, the jangling noise made by the apron when the legionaries marched helped to intimidate the enemy.

The heavy pendants weighed the leather strips down

Specially designed point of javelin would bend when pulled out of an enemy's shield

Woollen cloak

Leather bottle for water or wine

Pack for personal items and three days' rations

PIERCING POINTS
The thrusting spear of earlier times (left) was replaced by the fearsome heavy javelin, or *pilum* (right), which had a narrow point to pierce both shields and armor. A shower of these flying through the air would break the enemy's charge.

MARIUS'S MULE
A fully loaded legionary on the march carried more than armor, weapons, and a shield. Each man had a heavy pack held over the shoulder, which included a tool kit and a dish and pan. This burden weighed 90 lb (40 kg) or more, and often had to be carried up to 20 miles (30 km) in a day! Legionaries were called Marius's mules after the general who started the practice.

The sword's grip was often of wood, although bone and ivory were also used

The dagger had a double-edged blade

Mattock for digging ditches

Turf cutter for building turf ramparts

BOOTS MADE FOR WALKING
Military sandals (*caligae*) were as important as armor, because the legions won wars by fast marches as much as by battle. These boots were strong and well ventilated, with patterns of iron hobnails specially designed to take weight and withstand miles of marching.

SWORD AND DAGGER
A *pugio*, or dagger, was worn on the left, and *a gladius*, or short sword, on the right. Both were Spanish types, copied by the Romans. The sword was a terrible stabbing weapon, short enough to wield easily in the crush of battle. It was horribly effective against the mostly unarmored Gauls.

Battle and defense

B<small>Y THE BEGINNING</small> of the 1st century A.D., the Romans had acquired most of their empire; seas, deserts, mountains, and forests stopped them from going much farther. Only a few lands like Britain were added in the next hundred years. Now the soldiers were kept busy subduing uprisings and guarding the frontiers of the conquered provinces. Many of the wars at this time were fought to stop outsiders from invading the provinces. The legions remained the backbone of the army, but the auxiliary regiments (which included infantry and cavalry) became more and more important: it was their job to patrol and guard the thousands of miles of frontier that now existed around the Roman Empire.

CATAPULT BOLTS
Soldiers in the army used catapults to hurl darts and stones at the enemy. These are the iron tips from wooden darts or "bolts." Each legion had about 60 catapults, fearsome weapons used mostly in sieges.

A PROVINCE WON
Julius Caesar conquered Gaul in the 50s B.C., mainly for his own glory. Gallic resistance was finally crushed at the siege of Alesia, where Caesar trapped the Gallic leader Vercingetorix. This detail from a 19th-century painting shows the proud Gaul about to enter the Roman camp to surrender to Caesar, seated on a red platform in the distance.

AN AUXILIARY SOLDIER
Auxiliary soldiers supplemented the legions. Usually recruited from subject peoples of the empire, they were seldom citizens. This bronze statuette shows an auxiliary soldier wearing a mail shirt.

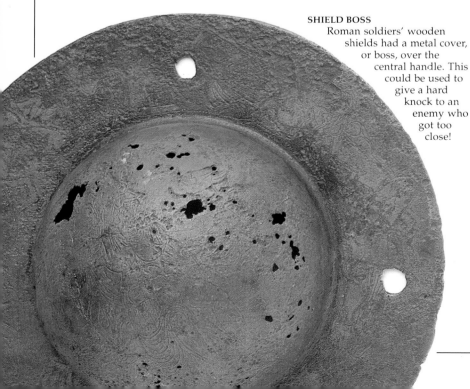

SHIELD BOSS
Roman soldiers' wooden shields had a metal cover, or boss, over the central handle. This could be used to give a hard knock to an enemy who got too close!

A ROMAN FORT
Soldiers spent the winter months, and times of peace, in timber or stone forts. On the left is the rebuilt gate of a fort at South Shields in northern England.

THE SPOILS OF WAR
An ivory plaque shows captured arms – one reward for taking over enemy territory. Plunder from conquests helped to finance the splendor of Rome, filled the emperor's coffers, and paid the troops. Rome's wars of conquest also brought several million slaves to Italy, from all over the empire.

SCALY PROTECTION
Fabric shirts covered with bronze scales were a common type of armor. Several thousand scales were stapled into rows and laced to the shirt.

The cavalry

The auxiliary cavalry were among the highest paid of Roman soldiers, partly because they had to pay for and equip their own horses. Italians were not very good horsemen, so the army raised regiments in areas where fighting on horseback was traditional, such as Gaul (ancient France), Holland, and Thrace (Bulgaria). The cavalry were the eyes of the army, patrolling and scouting ahead of the legions, guarding their flanks in battle, and pursuing defeated enemies.

A PARADE
A relief from Rome shows legionaries and galloping cavalrymen. Some of the cavalry carry standards, which were emblems of identification. The legionaries sport crests on top of their helmets (p. 10).

HARNESS FITTING
This is one of a set of fine silvered harness fittings from Xanten in Germany. Such showy equipment probably belonged to a cavalry officer.

CAVALRY SPUR
Riders used spurs attached to their shoes to urge their horses on. The stirrup had not yet been invented. Instead saddles had tall pommels, which gave riders a secure seat.

BATTLE WITH BARBARIANS
This wild entanglement of limbs, horses, and armor is a relief from a stone coffin showing Roman cavalry in combat with northern barbarians. Although the artist did not depict the soldiers very accurately, he gives a fine impression of the bloody chaos of battle.

SPEARHEADS
Auxiliary foot soldiers and horsemen used light javelins for throwing (p. 91), but heavier spears for thrusting at close range. Today only the iron spearheads survive; the wooden shafts rotted long ago. These examples come from Hod Hill in Dorset, England.

CHAMPING AT THE BIT
The Roman horse harness was basically the same as today. Leather reins and a bridle were linked to a bit which went into the horse's mouth. This one from Hod Hill is identical in form to modern snaffle bits.

Senators, citizens, subjects, and slaves

ROMAN SOCIETY had a very definite social scale. The people of the early empire were divided into Roman citizens, non-citizen provincials, and slaves. Citizens themselves were divided into different ranks, and had privileges that were denied to non-citizens. The senate in Rome, the heart of government since the Republic, was controlled by the emperor. Consuls, other magistrates, and provincial governors were chosen from its members – all wealthy men. The next rank of citizens, the equestrians, were also rich men who served in the army and administration. It was quite possible to change rank in Roman society: equestrians could become senators, and many Roman citizens had slave ancestors. Although some slaves were downtrodden, others were well treated and even powerful; for a long time the emperor's slaves and freedmen (ex-slaves) ran the civil service.

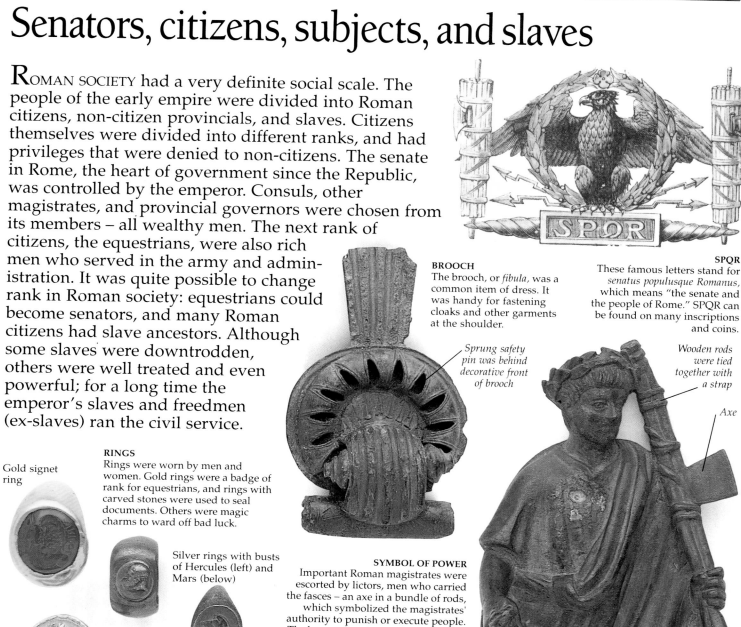

BROOCH
The brooch, or *fibula*, was a common item of dress. It was handy for fastening cloaks and other garments at the shoulder.

Sprung safety pin was behind decorative front of brooch

SPQR
These famous letters stand for *senatus populusque Romanus*, which means "the senate and the people of Rome." SPQR can be found on many inscriptions and coins.

Wooden rods were tied together with a strap

Axe

RINGS
Rings were worn by men and women. Gold rings were a badge of rank for equestrians, and rings with carved stones were used to seal documents. Others were magic charms to ward off bad luck.

Gold signet ring

Silver rings with busts of Hercules (left) and Mars (below)

Ring made out of a gold coin

SYMBOL OF POWER
Important Roman magistrates were escorted by lictors, men who carried the fasces – an axe in a bundle of rods, which symbolized the magistrates' authority to punish or execute people. The bronze figurine on the right dates to about the 1st century A.D.

Nobleman

Sacrificial assistant

Priest

Priest sacrificing

Peasant

MEN'S GEAR
Roman men wore a knee-length sleeveless tunic, perhaps with undergarments and various types of cloak. On formal occasions citizens wore the heavy white toga. Trousers were regarded as an unmanly foreign fashion!

Citizen in toga

Senator

HEADED PAPER
The back of this wooden writing tablet bears the brand of the procurator of the province of Britain. It was the "headed notepaper" of the official of equestrian rank who collected taxes and paid the army in Britain. The procurator was of a lower rank than the provincial governor, a senator who commanded the army and administered justice. Both officials were selected by the emperor, and had staffs of slaves and military clerks.

On the other side there was a layer of wax to write on (p. 118)

ESCAPE FROM THE ARENA
People were made slaves in various ways: by war, by the courts, and by being born to slave parents. Most gladiators were slaves, but success in the arena could win them their freedom. Above is the bone discharge ticket to freedom of a gladiator named Moderatus.

THE FORUM
Each Roman town had a forum – a market square with public buildings around it. The forum in Rome (above) was the heart of the capital, through which ran the Sacred Way to the Capitoline Hill and the temple of Jupiter. On the right of the picture is the *curia,* or senate house. Nearby were the imperial palace and the Colosseum.

Clipped beard fashionable around A.D. 130

CHANGING FASHIONS
Roman men were keen followers of fashion, especially hairstyles. The Roman gentleman shown in the bronze bust sports the thick hair and clipped beard fashionable around A.D. 130. Subsequently beards were allowed to grow longer and longer, until about A.D. 230, when stubbly beards and military crewcuts came into fashion.

The women of Rome

Silver distaff, used to hold wool or linen fibers being spun into thread

WOMEN IN ROME were expected to run the household (p. 100) and be dignified wives and good mothers. Girls received very little schooling, if any at all (p. 98). The degree of freedom a woman enjoyed had a lot to do with her wealth and status. Wealthy women, especially single women and widows who controlled their own property, had a good deal of independence. Wives of emperors and senators often had a lot of influence behind the scenes. At the other end of the scale, large numbers of women were slaves, ranging from ladies' maids to farm workers.

BUST OF A WOMAN
Above is a small silver bust probably from the center of a decorative dish. It may be a portrait of a great Roman lady.

Bone needle

Bronze needle for finer work

Modern-looking bronze thimble

Spinning and weaving

Most Roman clothing was made of wool or linen, and the jobs of spinning and weaving yarn and making clothes were traditional wifely tasks which wealthy women avoided. The emperor Augustus made his daughter Julia do them as an example to others to keep up the old Roman ways and to demonstrate wifely virtues. Julia hated it!

Cosmetics

Many Roman women used makeup. A pale complexion was fashionable, and it was achieved by applying powdered chalk or white lead. Red ocher was used for cheek and lip color, and eyes were made up with compounds based on ash or antimony. Some cosmetics were poisonous.

Silver spatula for mixing and applying cosmetics

WOMEN'S DRESS
Roman women wore an inner and an outer tunic of wool or linen, and sometimes a cloak. The wealthy wore lightweight imported fabrics like Chinese silk and Indian cotton.

Scent bottle carved from precious onyx

This wall painting shows a girl pouring perfume into a phial

Above is an ivory comb from a grave. It is inscribed "Modestina, farewell." The poor used wooden or bone combs – more to get rid of lice than to style their hair!

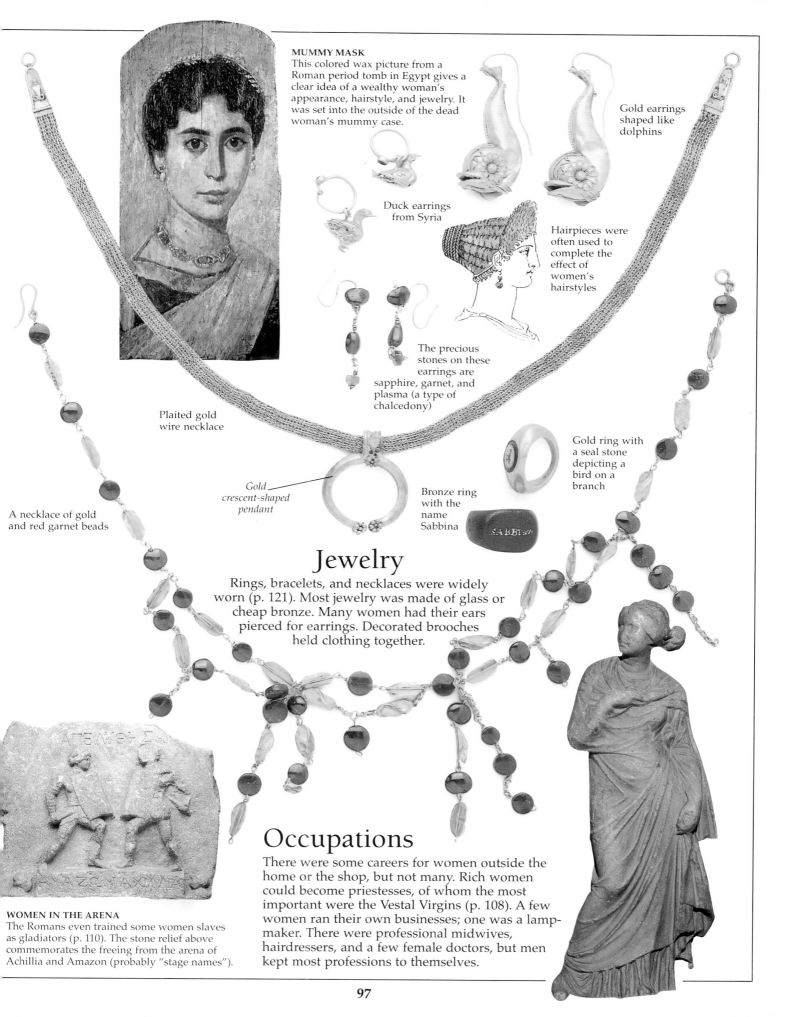

MUMMY MASK
This colored wax picture from a Roman period tomb in Egypt gives a clear idea of a wealthy woman's appearance, hairstyle, and jewelry. It was set into the outside of the dead woman's mummy case.

Gold earrings shaped like dolphins

Duck earrings from Syria

Hairpieces were often used to complete the effect of women's hairstyles

The precious stones on these earrings are sapphire, garnet, and plasma (a type of chalcedony)

Plaited gold wire necklace

Gold crescent-shaped pendant

Bronze ring with the name Sabbina

Gold ring with a seal stone depicting a bird on a branch

A necklace of gold and red garnet beads

Jewelry

Rings, bracelets, and necklaces were widely worn (p. 121). Most jewelry was made of glass or cheap bronze. Many women had their ears pierced for earrings. Decorated brooches held clothing together.

Occupations

There were some careers for women outside the home or the shop, but not many. Rich women could become priestesses, of whom the most important were the Vestal Virgins (p. 108). A few women ran their own businesses; one was a lamp-maker. There were professional midwives, hairdressers, and a few female doctors, but men kept most professions to themselves.

WOMEN IN THE ARENA
The Romans even trained some women slaves as gladiators (p. 110). The stone relief above commemorates the freeing from the arena of Achillia and Amazon (probably "stage names").

Growing up in Rome

"IS IT NEARLY OVER?"
Roman children dressed up just like their parents, and often accompanied them to official ceremonies. This detail from the Ara Pacis, a peace monument built by Augustus, shows members of the imperial family in a sacrificial procession. The children look rather unimpressed by the whole occasion!

FOR SOME LUCKY ROMAN CHILDREN, growing up consisted only of play and school. Roman fathers educated their own children until the time of the emperors, when those who could afford it hired tutors. Many also sent their children to school from the age of seven to learn the basics, with abacus and wax tablet. On the way to school children stopped at a breakfast bar as Italian children still do. School ran from dawn until noon; there was much learning by heart, and children were often thrashed when they made mistakes.

Girls rarely received more than a basic education after which they had to learn household skills from their mothers. Sons of the nobility would go on to prepare for a career in law or government. However, school was for the privileged few. Most children came from poor families; they could not read or write and were put to work at an early age.

YOUNG BOY
This realistic marble portrait bust depicts a young boy about five years old. The strange hair curl identifies him as a worshiper of Isis (p. 106).

Hair curl

SLEEPY SLAVE
Many Roman children were slaves. The oil flask (left) depicts a slave boy sitting on a box and dozing while he waits for his master to return. Many slaves were ill-treated and worked very long hours, so he may be taking a nap while he can. Perhaps his master is relaxing at the baths; this oil flask was probably used in bathing (p. 104).

LITTLE BOY'S LIFE
A marble relief from a sarcophagus shows scenes from the upbringing of a boy. On the left, the new-born infant is suckled by his mother and then is picked up by his father. Next the boy is shown with a donkey chariot. Finally he is seen reciting to his father.

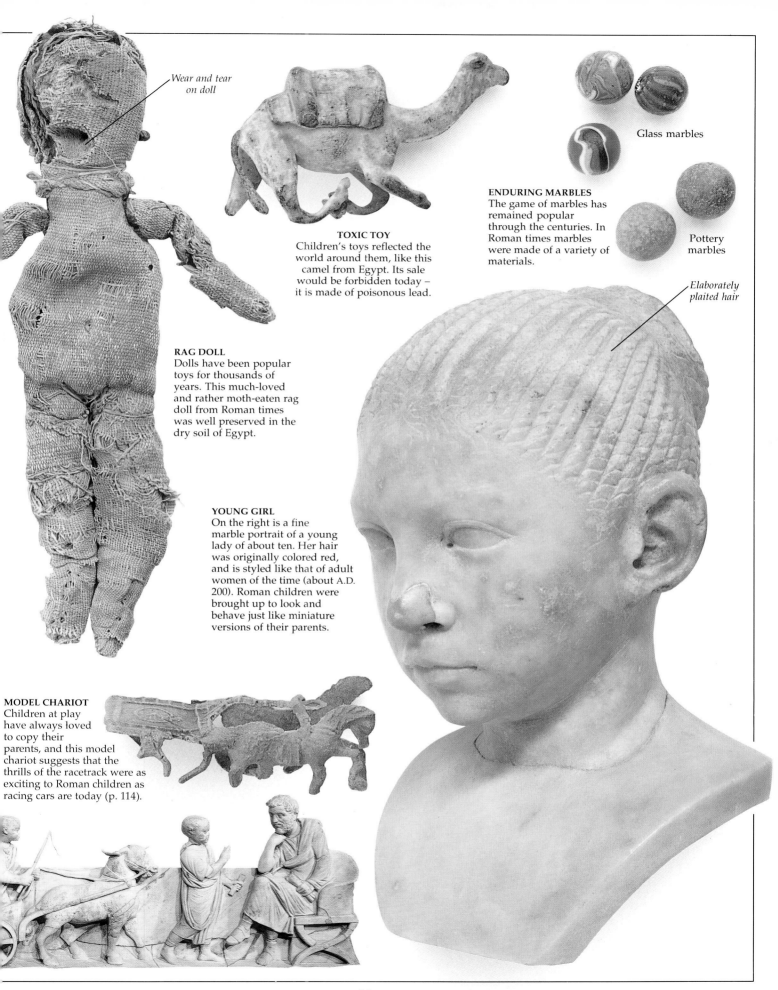

Wear and tear on doll

TOXIC TOY
Children's toys reflected the world around them, like this camel from Egypt. Its sale would be forbidden today – it is made of poisonous lead.

ENDURING MARBLES
The game of marbles has remained popular through the centuries. In Roman times marbles were made of a variety of materials.

Glass marbles

Pottery marbles

RAG DOLL
Dolls have been popular toys for thousands of years. This much-loved and rather moth-eaten rag doll from Roman times was well preserved in the dry soil of Egypt.

Elaborately plaited hair

YOUNG GIRL
On the right is a fine marble portrait of a young lady of about ten. Her hair was originally colored red, and is styled like that of adult women of the time (about A.D. 200). Roman children were brought up to look and behave just like miniature versions of their parents.

MODEL CHARIOT
Children at play have always loved to copy their parents, and this model chariot suggests that the thrills of the racetrack were as exciting to Roman children as racing cars are today (p. 114).

99

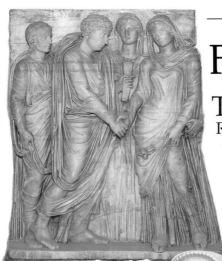

Family life

THE IDEA OF THE FAMILY was very important to the Romans, but they had a somewhat different understanding of the word than we do today. The paterfamilias, the father and head of the family, was traditionally all-powerful over the contents of his house – including all the people who lived in it, from wife to slave. He had, in theory, the power of life and death over his children. In practice, however, wives and children were not usually as downtrodden as this implies. His wife actually had her share of power, controlling the running of the house and its finances, and supervising the upbringing of the children until they were old enough to begin their schooling (p. 98). Larger households also had a number of slaves. Some were harshly treated, but others were some-times treated as members of the family.

A Roman wedding

In Roman times marriage took place often for financial or political reasons. On the wedding day the groom arrived with his family and friends at the bride's house, and the marriage took place in the atrium or at a nearby shrine. A sacrifice was offered, and the omens were read to make sure the gods approved. The bride and groom exchanged vows and clasped hands and so were married.

ENGAGEMENT RINGS
The groom often gave his future bride a ring with clasped hands, symbolizing marriage.

UNHAPPY FAMILY
This family portrait shows the emperor Septimus Severus with his wife and sons Caracalla and Geta. This imperial family was not a happy one; after Severus died, Caracalla murdered Geta before being killed himself. After this, his memory was officially cursed, and his portrait (above left) was defaced.

Slaves and pets

To modern eyes, wealthy Roman households would have seemed crowded and lacking in privacy, with slaves scurrying around cleaning, carrying things, and tending to the needs of the family. The household also included working animals: guard dogs, hunting dogs on country estates, perhaps horses, and cats to chase rats. There were also lap dogs, caged birds, and other pets, mainly for the children.

FREED SLAVE
Hedone, freed maidservant of Marcus Crassus, set up this bronze plaque to the goddess Feronia, who was popular with freed slaves.

SAD SLAVE?
Above right is a model of a kitchen slave weeping as he works at the *mortarium*. He is either unhappy with his hard life, or grinding up a strong onion!

GUARD DOG
There were many breeds of dog in the Roman Empire, including fierce guard dogs like the one on the right, kept chained at the door to deter thieves.

Dog collar

DOG TAG
Some Roman dogs wore identity tags in case they got lost. This bronze tag from a dog says "Hold me if I run away, and return me to my master Viventius on the estate of Callistus."

Household gods

Most Romans were religious and respected their many gods (p. 106), especially the particular gods and spirits who protected each home from evil. Every house had its own shrine, where the whole family worshiped daily. It was also very important to remember the family ancestors. Senatorial families kept wax masks or portraits of their ancestors, and most people would regularly go to the family graves to pay homage to the dead.

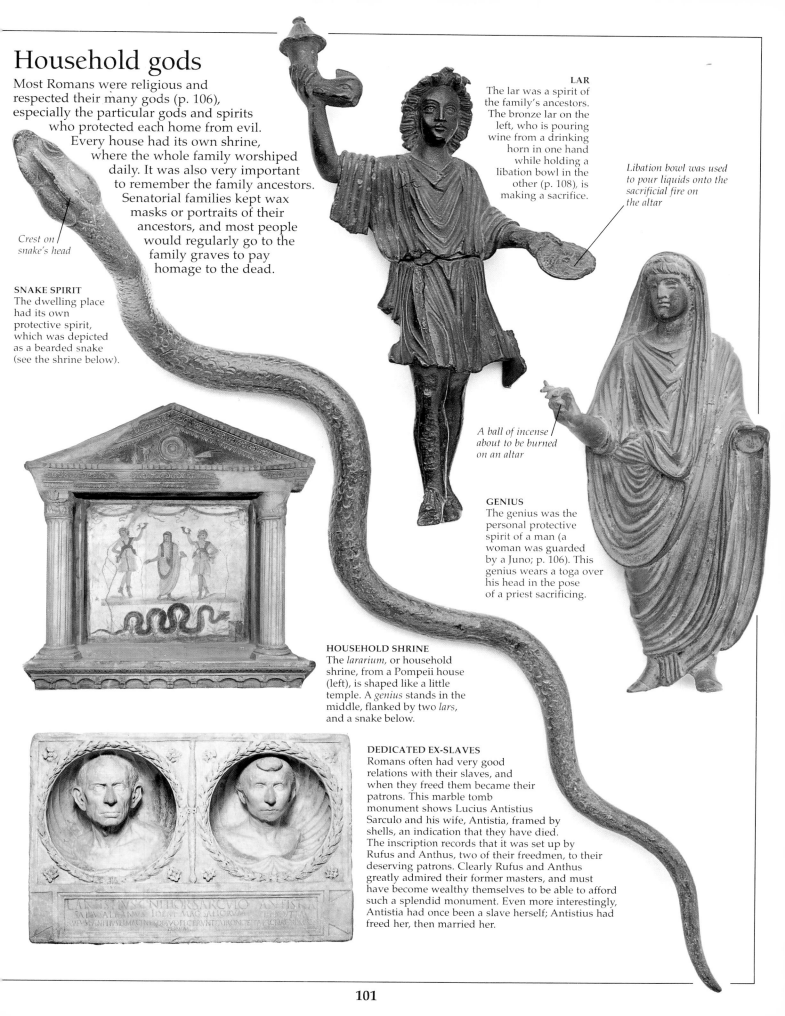

Crest on snake's head

SNAKE SPIRIT
The dwelling place had its own protective spirit, which was depicted as a bearded snake (see the shrine below).

LAR
The lar was a spirit of the family's ancestors. The bronze lar on the left, who is pouring wine from a drinking horn in one hand while holding a libation bowl in the other (p. 108), is making a sacrifice.

Libation bowl was used to pour liquids onto the sacrificial fire on the altar

A ball of incense about to be burned on an altar

GENIUS
The genius was the personal protective spirit of a man (a woman was guarded by a Juno; p. 106). This genius wears a toga over his head in the pose of a priest sacrificing.

HOUSEHOLD SHRINE
The *lararium*, or household shrine, from a Pompeii house (left), is shaped like a little temple. A *genius* stands in the middle, flanked by two *lars*, and a snake below.

DEDICATED EX-SLAVES
Romans often had very good relations with their slaves, and when they freed them became their patrons. This marble tomb monument shows Lucius Antistius Sarculo and his wife, Antistia, framed by shells, an indication that they have died. The inscription records that it was set up by Rufus and Anthus, two of their freedmen, to their deserving patrons. Clearly Rufus and Anthus greatly admired their former masters, and must have become wealthy themselves to be able to afford such a splendid monument. Even more interestingly, Antistia had once been a slave herself; Antistius had freed her, then married her.

Builders and engineers

T HE ROMANS were great builders, constructing temples, country houses, and magnificent public buildings of carved marble. Although they adopted many Greek architectural styles, they had their own trademarks. They invented the dome and made great use of arches. They used fired bricks and developed concrete by mixing *pozzolana*, a strong volcanic material, with rubble. Their structures had a long life span – even the mosaics they used in decorating are perfectly preserved in many places. Romans also had sound engineering skills; they brought water supplies to cities along aqueducts, and built roads and bridges that are in use to this day.

PONT DU GARD, FRANCE
A vast stone three-storied bridge carried an aqueduct over a gorge. The water flowed through a covered channel along the top. The aqueduct ran for about 30 miles (50 km), ending in a reservoir which supplied 22,000 tons of water to the city of Nîmes every day.

PLUMB BOB
A simple bronze weight on a string, called a plumb bob, gave a perfectly vertical line to make sure walls were straight. The owner's name, Bassus, is inscribed on the bob. Such simple tools were used to plan and build the Pont du Gard (above).

The foot-rule is divided into 12 Roman inches

BRONZE FOOT-RULE
This folding bronze rule was probably owned by a Roman stonemason or a carpenter, and was easily carried on a belt or in a bag. It is one Roman foot long (11 2/3 in; 296 mm).

The dividers are tightened with a wedge

BRONZE DIVIDERS
Proportional dividers like these were used by engineers when working with scale plans and models. The gap between the lower points is always twice that between the upper points, allowing, for example, statues to be copied at twice, or half, natural size.

BRONZE SQUARE
Used for checking the squareness of shapes, this tool would have been useful to carpenters, stone-masons, mosaic makers, and other craftsmen. It measures 90 and 45 degree angles.

A ROMAN ROAD
Roads were usually very straight, and carefully built with a camber (hump) so that rainwater drained off into ditches. This made the roads usable in all weather. Each road was made up of several levels, with a firm foundation. Gravel or stone slabs covered the surface.

CHISEL
Romans used chisels like this iron one when they worked with wood. Wood was used a lot in building, especially for roof frames, but, like this chisel's handle, most Roman wood has long since rotted.

Roman plumbing

The water supply system was very advanced in many Roman cities, more so than anything else until the 19th-century. The great aqueducts supplied many water outlets, including public fountains in the streets (from which most people fetched their domestic water in buckets). Bathhouses had their own supply (p. 104), as did public toilets. Larger private houses often had water from a main, and also collected rainwater from the roof. Elaborate systems of lead pipes fed the water to these places under gravity, and after use a system of underground sewers carried the waste away.

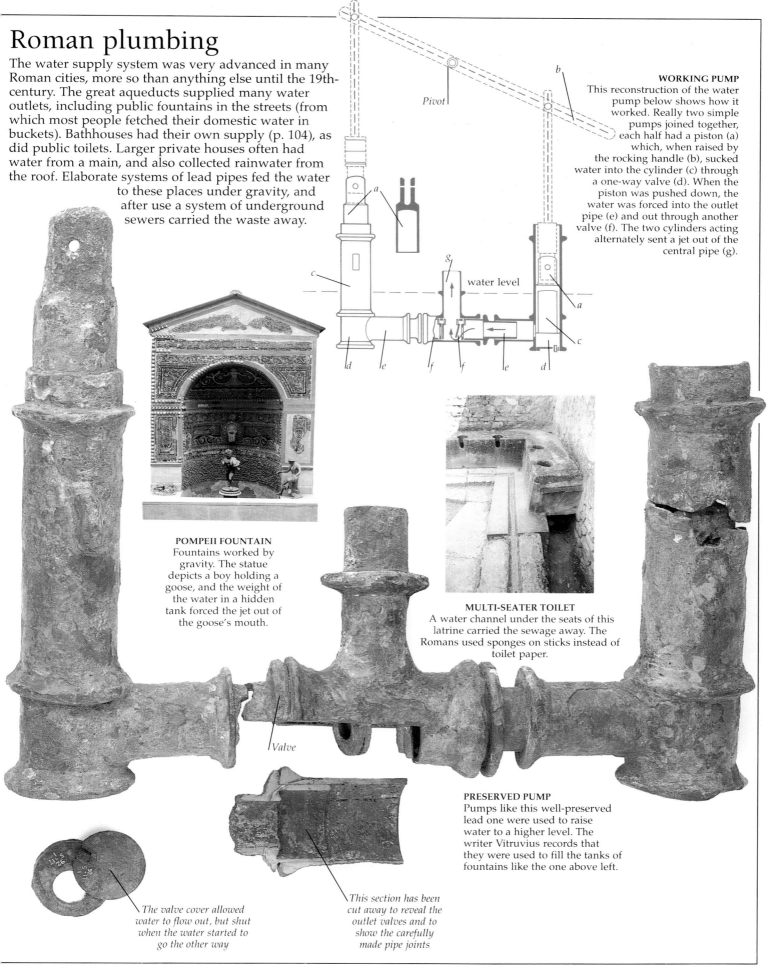

Pivot

WORKING PUMP
This reconstruction of the water pump below shows how it worked. Really two simple pumps joined together, each half had a piston (a) which, when raised by the rocking handle (b), sucked water into the cylinder (c) through a one-way valve (d). When the piston was pushed down, the water was forced into the outlet pipe (e) and out through another valve (f). The two cylinders acting alternately sent a jet out of the central pipe (g).

water level

POMPEII FOUNTAIN
Fountains worked by gravity. The statue depicts a boy holding a goose, and the weight of the water in a hidden tank forced the jet out of the goose's mouth.

MULTI-SEATER TOILET
A water channel under the seats of this latrine carried the sewage away. The Romans used sponges on sticks instead of toilet paper.

Valve

PRESERVED PUMP
Pumps like this well-preserved lead one were used to raise water to a higher level. The writer Vitruvius records that they were used to fill the tanks of fountains like the one above left.

The valve cover allowed water to flow out, but shut when the water started to go the other way

This section has been cut away to reveal the outlet valves and to show the carefully made pipe joints

A trip to the baths

FEW ROMAN HOUSES had their own baths; most people went to large public bathing establishments. These were not just places to get clean. Men went to the baths after a day's work to exercise, play games, meet friends, chat, and relax. Women went to their own separate baths, or used the public baths in the morning. Besides an exercise yard, or hall, there were the complicated bath buildings themselves. Changing rooms, where people left all their clothes on shelves, led to a series of progressively hotter chambers. The heat could be either dry (like a sauna) or steamy (like a Turkish bath), and the idea was to clean the pores of the skin by sweating. Soap was a foreign curiosity; olive oil was used instead. Afterward there were cold plunge-baths or swimming pools to close the pores. This might be followed by a relaxing massage, before going home for dinner.

Ivory counters for a board game

The inscription on the above counter means "bad luck"

Ivory (above), bone (above right), and glass gaming counters

Agate dice

Rock crystal dice

Metal dice shaped like squatting men

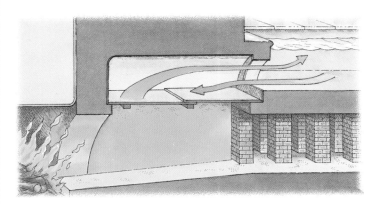

BATH HOUSE FOUNDATIONS
These foundations of a bath house were revealed in London, England, in 1989. The bottoms of the brick pillars which once supported the raised floor can be seen. Hot air circulating through this space heated the floor and the room above it (see below).

HEATING THE BATHS
Fires stoked by slaves from outside the bath building sent hot air under the floors and through hollow tiles in the walls to chimneys in the roof. The floors and walls became so hot that people inside had to wear wooden clogs to avoid burning their feet. The fires were also used to boil water in tanks and to heat pools, as the drawing on the left shows.

Games and gambling

People came to the baths to exercise and play in the yard, some perhaps training with weights, others playing ball games. These included catching games, which involved counting scores, and were played with colored balls of all sizes including heavy medicine balls. The less energetic bought drinks and snacks from vendors, or sat in the shade playing board games or gambling with dice (a favorite pastime of Augustus). Such games were also played in taverns and at home, away from the noise and bustle of the bath house.

THE BATHS AT BATH
The natural hot spring at Bath, England was used by the Romans as the center of a medical bathing complex. Sick people came from all over the country to seek a cure by swimming in the waters and praying to Sulis, the Celtic goddess of the place, whom the Romans identified with Minerva (p. 106). People still use the waters for their health-giving properties today.

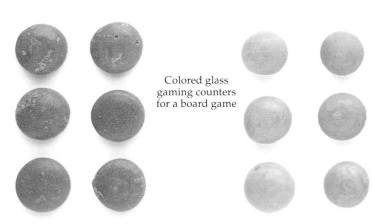

Colored glass gaming counters for a board game

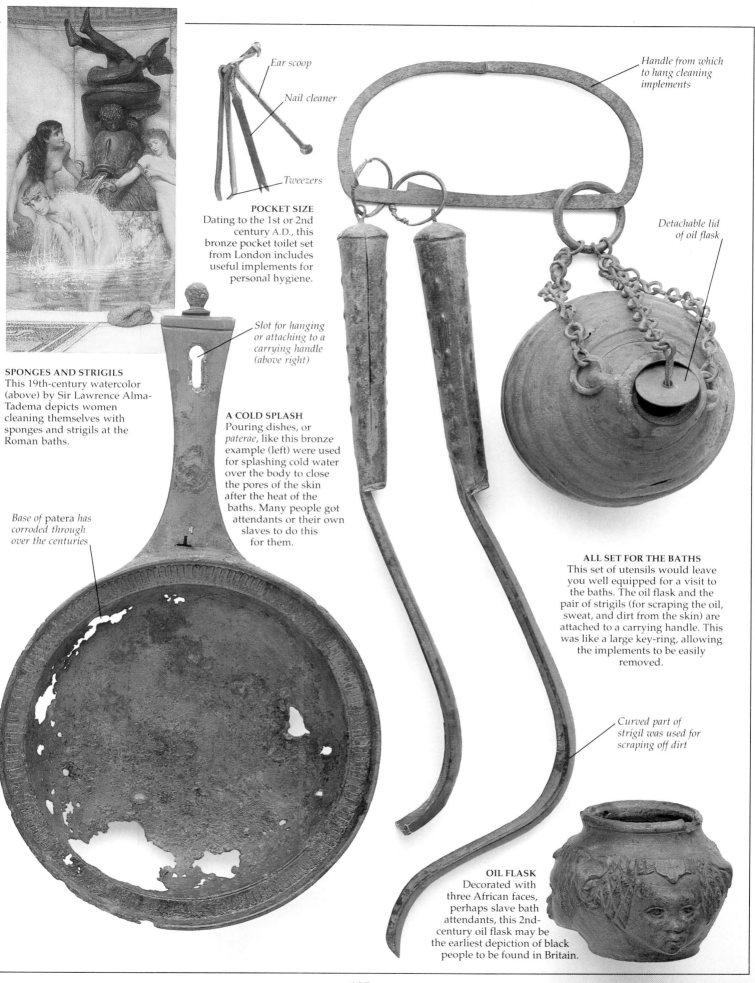

Ear scoop

Nail cleaner

Tweezers

POCKET SIZE
Dating to the 1st or 2nd century A.D., this bronze pocket toilet set from London includes useful implements for personal hygiene.

Handle from which to hang cleaning implements

Detachable lid of oil flask

Slot for hanging or attaching to a carrying handle (above right)

SPONGES AND STRIGILS
This 19th-century watercolor (above) by Sir Lawrence Alma-Tadema depicts women cleaning themselves with sponges and strigils at the Roman baths.

A COLD SPLASH
Pouring dishes, or *paterae*, like this bronze example (left) were used for splashing cold water over the body to close the pores of the skin after the heat of the baths. Many people got attendants or their own slaves to do this for them.

Base of patera has corroded through over the centuries

ALL SET FOR THE BATHS
This set of utensils would leave you well equipped for a visit to the baths. The oil flask and the pair of strigils (for scraping the oil, sweat, and dirt from the skin) are attached to a carrying handle. This was like a large key-ring, allowing the implements to be easily removed.

Curved part of strigil was used for scraping off dirt

OIL FLASK
Decorated with three African faces, perhaps slave bath attendants, this 2nd-century oil flask may be the earliest depiction of black people to be found in Britain.

105

A world of many gods

Across the Roman Empire people worshiped hundreds of different gods and goddesses, demigods (half gods), and spirits. These were depicted as large human forms, like the Greek gods. Everyone was expected to offer sacrifices to the important gods of the Roman state, such as Jupiter, and to the guardian spirit of the emperor. Many worshiped at the shrine of their local deity or chose foreign gods who offered comfort and hope for the afterlife – for example, Mithras or Isis. There were gods to protect the house; gods of healing; in fact gods of all aspects of life. Generally people tolerated the beliefs of others. However, the Christians were an important exception. Their beliefs prevented them from sacrificing to the Roman gods, and so they were thought to be dangerous unbelievers who imperiled Rome by offending the gods. As a result, the Christians were persecuted from time to time by the Romans (p. 112).

GOD OF THUNDER
The king of the Roman gods was Jupiter, known as Best and Greatest, a sky god whose symbols were the eagle and the thunderbolt. Jupiter was a lot like the Greek god Zeus. His main home was the great temple on the Capitoline Hill in Rome.

WOMEN'S GODDESS
Juno, the wife of Jupiter, was the patron goddess of women. The clay figurine above shows her enthroned with a peacock, her symbol.

TEMPLE OF AUGUSTUS AND LIVIA
Most emperors were declared gods after their deaths, and temples were built at which to worship them. Augustus and his wife, Livia (p. 89), were made into gods. The well-preserved temple which still stands in Vienne, France, was built in their honor. Many Roman temples looked like this. Each temple was thought of as the home of the god or goddess it was dedicated to. Offerings were made at an altar in front of the building.

EGYPTIAN GODS
Some Romans worshiped mysterious foreign gods, as well as their own traditional ones. The Egyptian goddess Isis (left) was one of the most popular of these, and was worshiped with the god Serapis (above). The religion was about the cycle of life, death, and rebirth, and its secret ceremonies gave worshipers a sense of belonging and hope for the next world.

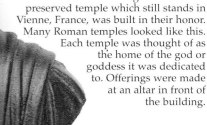

WISE GODDESS
Warlike Minerva, with her helmet and armor, was very much like the famous Greek goddess Athena. Minerva was the goddess of handicrafts and wisdom. She is often depicted on soldiers' armor.

MARS AND VENUS
Mars, the god of war, is still remembered in the name of the month March. Gauls and Britons came to worship many of their own gods as versions of similar Roman ones, usually Mars or Mercury, the messenger of the gods (p. 109). The silver plaque from Britain on the right is dedicated to a Romano-British "mixed" god called Mars Alator. Venus, the Roman goddess of love, beauty, and fertility, was said to be the divine ancestor of the family of Julius Caesar.

Gilded silver plaque was a temple offering

Inscription says that the plaque was given to fulfill a promise to the god

Julius Caesar built a temple to Venus in Rome

GOD OF LIGHT
Mithraism was a Persian cult concerned with the eternal struggle of good and evil. Mithras was worshiped by many soldiers – it was a "men only" religion. The statue shows Mithras slaying the bull whose blood gave life to the universe.

A RIOTOUS GOD
Also called Dionysus, Bacchus was a Greek god who promised rebirth to his followers. He was also the god of wine, so not surprisingly his festivals could be riotous! Theater started as part of his worship.

Bacchus holds bunches of grapes as a symbol of wine

Busts of the gods decorate the clamps

THE CULT OF CYBELE
Cybele was a mother goddess from Turkey. Her religion was about fertility and the cycle of death and rebirth. It was a very emotional religion, and sometimes her priests would work themselves into a frenzy and castrate themselves for her. These bronze clamps may have been used for this gruesome ritual.

The monster is eating a man

GOAT GOD
One of many Greek gods adopted by Rome, Pan was a son of Hermes (Mercury). Half man, half goat, he was a god of mountains and lonely places, of flocks and shepherds, and he played panpipes. He could cause herds of animals to "panic" and stampede.

CELTIC GOD
The Britons and Gauls believed in some grim gods, like this monster, and sacrificed people to them.

Worship and sacrifice

PEOPLE FEARED THE GODS and sought to win their favor or ask for their help. People would pray and make offerings at temples to seek divine favors or to give thanks afterward. Offerings came in all shapes and sizes, from coins and brooches left by the poor, to silver statues donated by the rich. Augustus promised Mars a new temple if the god helped him to avenge the death of Caesar, and today the remains of the Temple of Mars the Avenger can still be seen in Rome. People also sacrificed food and drink, and burned incense on altars. Animal sacrifices were common, ranging from a single bird to a whole herd of cattle. There were few full-time priests or priestesses, except for the Vestal Virgins, who guarded the holy flame of the goddess Vesta in Rome. Most priests were important people in public life for whom a priesthood was one of many duties. The emperor was chief priest of Rome. The title was Pontifex Maximus, or chief bridge builder, because he bridged the space between the people and the gods.

PRIESTESS SACRIFICING
A priestess pours a libation (probably milk, oil, or wine) onto an altar as an offering to a goddess or god. In a number of religions women were the only or the main worshipers. The cults of Vesta, Isis, and Cybele were particularly associated with women.

LIBATION JUG
A bronze jug such as this was used for holding liquids to pour during sacrifices. The jug, bowl, and knife are often shown in religious scenes with other priestly gear.

Lion-headed handle

UNDER THE KNIFE
Animals were sacrificed in various ways; larger beasts like cattle were felled with an axe. Then a knife was used to slit the animal's throat and cut it open. Its inner organs were removed for the priests to study (see opposite page).

LIBATION BOWL
A libation bowl was used to pour liquids into the fire on top of the altar. The smoke from this and from the burned flesh would ascend to the heavens to please the god.

CURSE TABLET
One way to seek revenge on enemies was to place a curse on them at the local temple. This lead plaque from the temple at Uley in Gloucestershire, England, asks Mercury to make the thieves who stole a valuable animal fall sick until they return it.

THE BARE BONES
Certain animals were chosen to be sacrificed to certain gods. Mercury's "holy animals" were the cock and the ram, and the many thousands of bones found at Uley show that people sacrificed sheep and chickens in his honor there. Above are some of the chicken bones.

OFFERING A SACRIFICE
On this relic from Italy a silenus, or Greek woodland spirit, is shown making an offering at an altar. Sileni were companions of the god Bacchus (Dionysus, p. 107). You can see the fire on the altar and the libation being poured.

DIVINE MESSENGER
Above is a little bronze statue of Mercury, messenger of the gods, which was left as an offering at his temple at Uley. Perhaps it was a thank-you offering for a favor granted, or a gift and a reminder of a request not yet fulfilled.

LIVER IN THE HAND
A fragment of a marble statue shows a hand holding an animal's liver. A special priest with the Etruscan title *haruspex* would read the god's will from the liver's shape and condition. It was thought to be a bad sign if the organ was deformed in any way.

The way that the sacred chickens ate showed whether or not the gods approved of a plan

BOAR TO THE SLAUGHTER
An attendant leads a boar to the altar for sacrifice. Its inner organs would be burned on the altar as offerings to the gods, while the good meat was cooked for the faithful in a sacrificial meal. Roman religion could be very practical!

SACRIFICIAL ALTAR
Roman altars stood in the open, outside the front of the temple. The cult figure of the god was kept inside.

Mortal combat

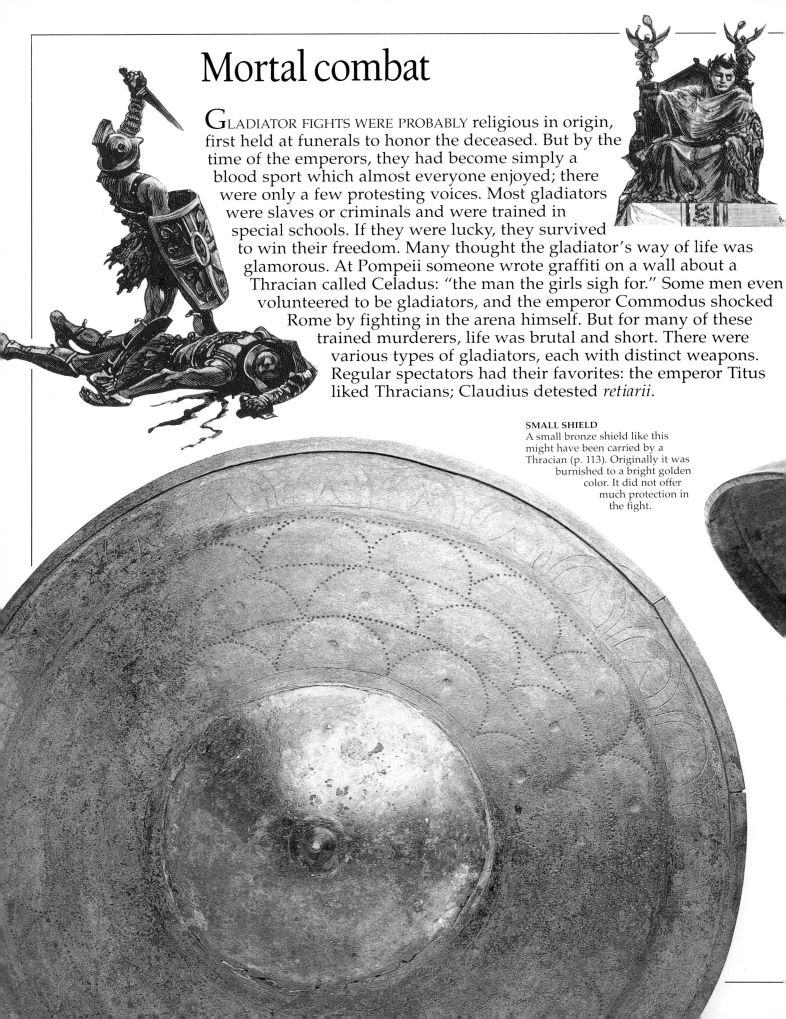

GLADIATOR FIGHTS WERE PROBABLY religious in origin, first held at funerals to honor the deceased. But by the time of the emperors, they had become simply a blood sport which almost everyone enjoyed; there were only a few protesting voices. Most gladiators were slaves or criminals and were trained in special schools. If they were lucky, they survived to win their freedom. Many thought the gladiator's way of life was glamorous. At Pompeii someone wrote graffiti on a wall about a Thracian called Celadus: "the man the girls sigh for." Some men even volunteered to be gladiators, and the emperor Commodus shocked Rome by fighting in the arena himself. But for many of these trained murderers, life was brutal and short. There were various types of gladiators, each with distinct weapons. Regular spectators had their favorites: the emperor Titus liked Thracians; Claudius detested *retiarii*.

SMALL SHIELD
A small bronze shield like this might have been carried by a Thracian (p. 113). Originally it was burnished to a bright golden color. It did not offer much protection in the fight.

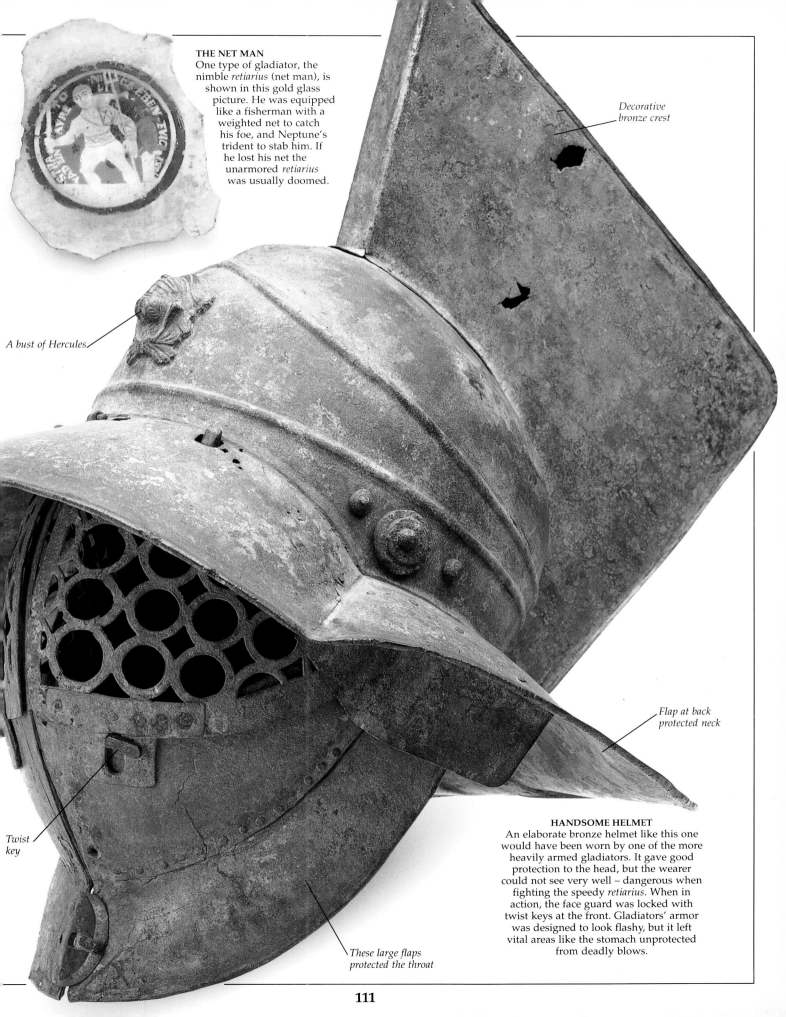

THE NET MAN
One type of gladiator, the nimble *retiarius* (net man), is shown in this gold glass picture. He was equipped like a fisherman with a weighted net to catch his foe, and Neptune's trident to stab him. If he lost his net the unarmored *retiarius* was usually doomed.

Decorative bronze crest

A bust of Hercules

Flap at back protected neck

Twist key

HANDSOME HELMET
An elaborate bronze helmet like this one would have been worn by one of the more heavily armed gladiators. It gave good protection to the head, but the wearer could not see very well – dangerous when fighting the speedy *retiarius*. When in action, the face guard was locked with twist keys at the front. Gladiators' armor was designed to look flashy, but it left vital areas like the stomach unprotected from deadly blows.

These large flaps protected the throat

Continued from previous page

Steel and claws

The games in the amphitheater lasted all day. In the morning wild animals were brought on to fight each other or to face "huntsmen," or simply to kill defenseless criminals. Some Christian martyrs died this way, although no definite cases are recorded of this in the Colosseum. Around midday there would be a break for the bodies to be removed and fresh sand spread while excitement rose in anticipation of the main attraction in the afternoon: the gladiators.

ELEPHANT
In their endless quest for novelty in the arena, the Romans scoured the known world for exotic animals like this African elephant.

BOUND FOR DEATH
All sorts of animals from foreign lands, like this antelope, were captured and put on ships bound for Rome and the Colosseum. It was so important to the emperors to put on lavish spectacles that they spent vast sums on this horrible trade.

Unprotected shoulder

Leopard is lunging at protected part of arm

"THE BRUTE TAMER OF POMPEII"
The Victorians were as fascinated as anyone by the horrors of the arena. This 19th-century lion tamer used "Roman" costume as a gimmick in his act.

BEAR
Bears were to be found within the empire for entertainment in the arena, and sometimes rarer animals from beyond the Roman world were obtained. These included polar bears, Indian tigers, and rhinoceroses.

SURPRISE ATTACK
A clay plaque shows a leopard springing at an unwary *bestiarius* (animal fighter). Some of the huntsmen liked to show off by fighting big cats while on stilts, but the spectators enjoyed watching the hunters die as much as they liked to see the animals being killed; it was all part of the "fun."

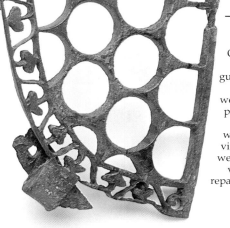

DEADLY DESIGNS
On the left is part of the intricate face guard of a gladiator's helmet. The holes were small enough to protect the face from sword and trident without blocking the view too much. If the wearer was killed, the valuable armor was repaired and passed on to another man.

THE FINAL MOMENT
The last tense moment of a fight is shown on this oil lamp. A wounded gladiator stares death in the face as the victor stands over him ready to deliver the final blow.

Shoulder guard to protect the neck

The gladiators
"We who are about to die salute you!" shouted the gladiators to the emperor, and the fighting began, to musical accompaniment. Several pairs or groups fought at a time. When a gladiator was wounded he could appeal for mercy. The emperor listened to the crowd's opinion; had the gladiator fought well enough to be spared? If not, the people jabbed downward with their thumbs, and he was killed.

A LIFE IN THE BALANCE
A bronze statuette of one of the heavily armed gladiators shows his armor on head, arms, and legs, and his unprotected stomach. His shield stands on the ground. He is probably wounded and appears to be raising his left hand in an appeal to be spared.

Curved sword

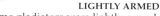

LIGHTLY ARMED
Some gladiators were lightly armed, as shown in these bronze figurines. On the left is a Thracian carrying a curved dagger and a very small shield; on the right is a *retiarius* (p. 111).

SCREEN GLADIATOR
The motion picture *Spartacus* brought the terror of the arena back to life. Here, Spartacus himself, armed as a Thracian (although without a helmet), fights a *retiarius*. He has lost his shield and has grabbed his foe's net to avoid being tripped.

DUEL TO THE DEATH
A clay plaque shows two heavily armed gladiators fighting it out, one thrusting at his opponent's neck, the other going for the vulnerable abdomen.

A day at the races

ALL OVER THE ROMAN EMPIRE, people flocked to see the "races" in their spare time. A day at the races meant a day spent betting on teams, cheering, and buying snacks from vendors. In an atmosphere charged with excitement, chariots creaked and horses stamped in the starting boxes. At the drop of a white cloth, the starting signal, the gates flew open, and the horses were off in a cloud of dust, thundering around the *spina* or central barrier. The audience went wild, cheering their chosen team – in the capital, the four teams were the Blues, Greens, Reds, and Whites, owned by the emperor. People followed their favorite teams and drivers with the passion of modern sports fans everywhere. Sometimes rivalry between fans led to violence. Fighting between the Blues and the Greens in Constantinople in A.D. 532 developed into a rebellion against the government in which thousands died.

WATCHING THE SHOW
This mosaic shows people watching the races. Here, men and women could sit together, unlike at other shows. The poet Ovid records that the racetrack was a good place to meet a boyfriend or a girlfriend

THE WINNER
A victorious charioteer (above) received a victor's palm and a purse of gold, and was hailed as a hero.

Chariots were very light for maximum speed

BEN HUR
The epic film *Ben Hur* tried to capture the excitement and danger of a charioteer's life. Controlling a *quadriga* – four horses at full gallop – was quite a task, especially on the turns, which held a special peril. At these, many charioteers took a tumble.

CHARIOT AND HORSE
Chariots called *bigae* were pulled by two horses; *quadrigae* had four horses. Special stables housed the trained racehorses. This bronze model is of a *biga*; one of the horses is missing. Races consisted of up to 12 chariots running seven laps, a total of about 5 miles (8 km). There were frequent crashes, injuries, and deaths, but they just added to the excitement of the hard-bitten racegoers. Chariots that had lost their drivers could still win a race if they crossed the line first.

Ram's head finial on top of chariot pole

ONE MAN AND HIS HORSE
This charioteer from the Blues team wears a leather harness to protect him in a fall. Successful charioteers often became very famous. And although mostly slaves, they sometimes made enough money to buy their freedom. Their racehorses had names like Candidus (Snowy), Rapax (Greedy), and Sagitta (Arrow).

Champion stallions were used for breeding during their racing years

POLE END
This bronze finial, or chariot pole decoration, shows a figure of a triton (merman). Chariots were built for looks as well as speed and could be splendidly decorated.

The triton blows a seashell trumpet

RECONSTRUCTED RACETRACK
The greatest racetrack of all, the Circus Maximus in Rome, seated up to 250,000 people. The chariots erupted from the starting gates set up on the long straight and thundered round in an counterclockwise direction. Seven laps later, the survivors crossed the finish line opposite the imperial box, on the left.

115

The theater

THE ROMANS largely copied theater from Greece, and the best actors of Roman plays were usually Greek. Stage shows were first put on as part of religious festivals, and were later paid for by the wealthy to gain popularity. Tickets were free – if you could get them. Although Romans of all classes enjoyed the plays, they thought the actors were a scandalous lot. Women were not allowed to sit near the front, in case they were tempted to run off with one of the performers! In writing comedies Roman playwrights like Plautus imitated Greek play scripts. The stories were about people like kidnapped heiresses, foolish old men, and cunning slaves, and usually had a happy ending. Roman audiences preferred comedies to tragedies. The Romans also invented their own types of performance, such as mime. Another Roman form, called pantomime, involved one actor dancing and miming a story from Greek legend to an accompaniment of singing and music.

MOSAIC MASKS
Roman actors were men (women could appear only in mimes), and they wore elaborate masks, like these in a mosaic from Rome. The masks indicated the sorts of characters portrayed, both young and old, male and female, gods and heroes. They were lightweight, but hot to wear.

A COMIC ACTOR
The cheeky, scheming slave was one of the standard characters of Roman comedy. When his plans were found out, he often ended up taking refuge in a temple, sitting on the altar, like the bronze figure above. Here he was safe from his pursuers until he moved!

TRAGIC FACE
Theater masks were favorite themes in Roman art. On the left is a marble carving of a female tragic mask. Actual masks were probably made of shaped and stiffened linen. There was a gaping mouth for the actor to speak through, and holes for him to see through.

A TROUPE OF PLAYERS
A mosaic, now in Naples, Italy, shows a group of actors in costumes and masks, dancing and playing musical instruments. The piper is dressed as a woman and is wearing the white mask of a female character.

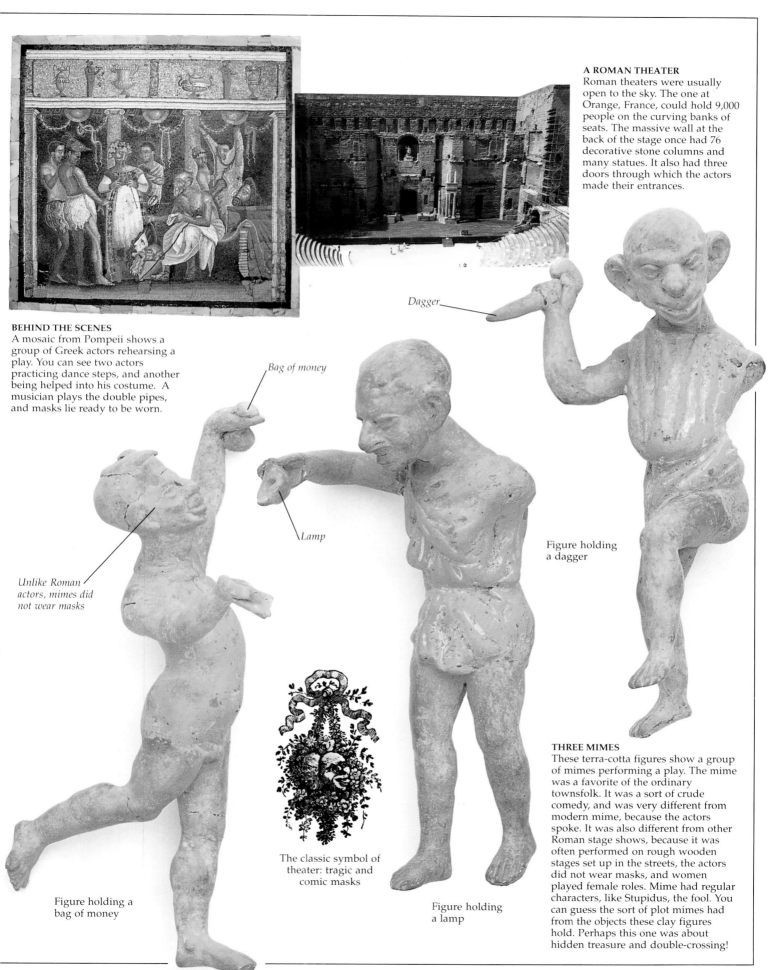

A ROMAN THEATER
Roman theaters were usually open to the sky. The one at Orange, France, could hold 9,000 people on the curving banks of seats. The massive wall at the back of the stage once had 76 decorative stone columns and many statues. It also had three doors through which the actors made their entrances.

Dagger

BEHIND THE SCENES
A mosaic from Pompeii shows a group of Greek actors rehearsing a play. You can see two actors practicing dance steps, and another being helped into his costume. A musician plays the double pipes, and masks lie ready to be worn.

Bag of money

Lamp

Figure holding a dagger

Unlike Roman actors, mimes did not wear masks

The classic symbol of theater: tragic and comic masks

Figure holding a bag of money

Figure holding a lamp

THREE MIMES
These terra-cotta figures show a group of mimes performing a play. The mime was a favorite of the ordinary townsfolk. It was a sort of crude comedy, and was very different from modern mime, because the actors spoke. It was also different from other Roman stage shows, because it was often performed on rough wooden stages set up in the streets, the actors did not wear masks, and women played female roles. Mime had regular characters, like Stupidus, the fool. You can guess the sort of plot mimes had from the objects these clay figures hold. Perhaps this one was about hidden treasure and double-crossing!

117

Writing it all down

DOZENS OF TONGUES were spoken across the Roman Empire, but Latin in the west and Greek in the east were the languages spoken and written for international communication, government, and trade. The Romans introduced writing to northern Europe for the first time, and the Latin alphabet is still used there. There were only 22 letters in this alphabet (I and J were not distinguished, nor were U and V; W and Y did not exist). Millions of texts were written, from great stone inscriptions to private letters scrawled on wax tablets, from elegant poems and histories carefully inked on papyrus scrolls to trade accounts scratched on broken pots. The tiny amount of texts that have survived are very precious because they contain information that ruined buildings and broken pots do not; writing is the only medium through which the Romans can still "speak" to us, about themselves and their world, about politics and what they thought and believed. But despite the importance of writing, most ordinary people were illiterate because of lack of education (p. 98) and because, in a world without printing, books had to be copied by hand, and so were rare and expensive.

ROMAN HANDWRITING
Everyday handwriting was very different from the familiar capitals seen on inscriptions. This is a fragment of a letter in Latin, written in ink on a wooden tablet, preserved in a waterlogged pit at the fort of Vindolanda near Hadrian's Wall. Addressed to a decurion (like a corporal) named Lucius, it is about a welcome gift of oysters from a friend of the writer.

TRAJAN'S COLUMN
The inscription on the base of Trajan's Column in Rome is a famous example of beautifully proportioned Roman capitals which were painted on walls as well as carved in stone like these. This example has served as a model for Roman-style typefaces for several hundred years.

SOOTY INK
Fine soot was mixed with water and other ingredients to make ink, which was used for writing on papyrus, wood, or parchment.

ROMAN NUMERALS
Unlike the Arabic numbers we use today, Roman numerals were written as strings of symbols to be added together, with I for 1, V for 5, X for 10, C for 100, and so on. Large numbers were quite clumsy and complicated; for example, 1,778 in Roman numerals is MDCCLXXVIII. This made arithmetic very difficult.

WAXING LYRICAL
Beeswax was melted and poured into shallow cavities in wooden tablets to form a reusable writing surface.

The number four can be IV or IIII

Roman numerals are still used on some modern clocks and watches

BLUE INKPOT
On the right is an inkpot from Egypt dating from the 1st century A.D. It is made of faience (a glassy material).

Vellum

A PAIR OF WRITERS
These portraits from Pompeii show a woman with a wax tablet and stylus and a man with a papyrus scroll. The tablet has two leaves which folded together to protect the writing. Roman books consisted of one or more scrolls; books with pages were invented during late Roman times.

INLAID INKPOTS
Expensive inkpots to grace the desks of the wealthy were an opportunity for craftsworkers to display their skills (p. 120). On the left is a bronze example with elegant silver inlay and a lid to stop the ink from drying up. Below is a pair of bronze inkpots, covered with black niello (silver or copper sulfide) and inlaid with silver and gold depicting mythological scenes.

Bronze stylus from Athens

Spatula end for smoothing the wax to erase writing

Iron stylus with bronze cover

HANGING INKPOT
Cords were once attached to the holes in this pottery inkpot and used for hanging or carrying.

Bronze pen

Reed pen with split nib

Ivory stylus

PENS AND STYLI
Split-nib pens of reed and metal were used with ink to write on vellum, papyrus, or wood. The pointed stylus was designed for writing on wax tablets.

Papyrus

PAPYRUS AND VELLUM
Routine texts were written on reusable wax tablets or cheap thin leaves of wood. Egyptian papyrus (paper made from reed fibers) was used for more important documents like legal contracts. The finest books were written on vellum, sheets of wafer-thin animal skin (usually kid or lamb) which had a beautiful writing surface and great durability.

119

Craftsworkers and technology

ROMAN OBJECTS WHICH SURVIVE TODAY show that people were enormously skilled at working in all sorts of materials. Pottery was a large-scale industry in some areas, where wine jars (p. 122) and red Samian pots were made by the million in large workshops. Many of the potters were slaves or freedmen, and surviving names show that they, and other craftsworkers, were almost all men. Other crafts were on a much smaller scale, with individual artisans working from their own shops in towns like Pompeii. In those days skills were developed through trial and error to see what worked. Sons learned from their fathers, slaves from their masters or foremen; there were no college courses. Particularly talented craftsworkers, even if they were slaves, might hope to make their fortune with specially commissioned pieces for rich clients.

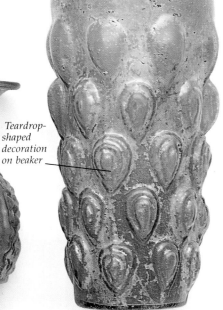

Face on flask

Teardrop-shaped decoration on beaker

FACE FLASK
This mass-produced flask was probably used for holding a cosmetic. It was made by blowing a bubble of glass into a mold.

MOLDED BEAKER
Mold blowing was the technique used to make this glass beaker. The mold had the teardrop decoration on the inside.

Glassworking

Glass had been made for centuries, but in the last century B.C. someone discovered that it was possible to blow glass into bubbles which could be formed quickly and cheaply into all kinds of useful vessels. Soon glass was being blown into molds, allowing mass production of bottles and highly decorated flasks. Glass was no longer a luxury, but became a widely used material. Sometimes broken glass was collected for recycling, as it is today.

BLUE RIBBED BOWL
Probably made by the older technique of pressing hot glass into a mold, this ribbed bowl is made of expensive blue glass. It may have been used as formal tableware at dinner parties.

Glass jar

Bands of gold running through the glass

Lid of jar

COLORFUL GLASS
Bands of colored glass and gold were incorporated into some vessels, like this delicate little jar and lid. It probably graced an elegant woman's dressing table (p. 96) and was used to store an expensive cosmetic.

PORTLAND VASE
A blown glass vessel, the Portland Vase is one of the most precious objects to survive from Roman times. A layer of white glass over the blue core was cut away with great skill to leave the elegant scenes of figures and foliage in white on a blue background. The task was probably performed by a jeweler, using the cameo technique developed to cut similar pictures from banded stone (p. 9). The procedure took many months. Such a famous work of art may well have belonged to the emperor – few others could have afforded it.

Metalwork and jewelry

Gold, silver, lead, copper, iron, and other metals were widely used by the Romans. Mining, extracting metal from ore, and melting the metal to pour into molds were also understood. The Romans could not make furnaces hot enough to melt iron, so they forged it, hammering it into shape while it was hot. Metals were mixed to make alloys such as bronze, a mixture of copper and tin. Roman bronze often contained zinc as well, giving it a gold color.

Boneworking

Bone was the plastic of the ancient world, used for making many everyday items such as knife handles, hairpins, and combs. It was also widely used for sword hilts. Fresh animal bone from the butcher's could be finely carved, and was also used for inlays on wooden boxes. Gaming counters and dice were frequently carved from bone (p. 104).

SILVER MIRROR
Mirror glass had not yet been invented, so the Romans used polished metal instead. This polished silver mirror is attached to a separately made handle in the form of the club and lionskin of Hercules (the mythical Greek hero).

Woman's head on end of hairpin

Outline of figure which was originally inlaid with gold foil

Curved blade of knife

BONE PINS
Large needles and pins were among the most common objects made from bone. These three are from Colchester, England. Hairpins were often necessary for the elaborate hairstyles worn by Roman women (p. 19).

BRONZE PLAQUE
This small sheet of bronze bears a delicate gold foil inlay set into its surface. Outlines of figures were made before the inlaying took place.

SMITH'S TOOLS
The iron tongs were probably used by a smith to heat fairly small metal objects in a furnace.

BONE-HANDLED KNIFE
Roman knives were often of this type, with a carved bone handle and a loop for hanging.

Loop for hanging knife up

BONE COMB
Most Roman combs were made like this one. The teeth were cut with a very fine saw.

JEWELER'S HOARD
These silver objects are part of a large hoard of jewelry, coins, and scrap silver that was buried at Snettisham, England, in the second century A.D. They represent the stock of materials and finished work of a silversmith.

Another tool of the trade, this iron file has lost its wooden handle

RINGS
There were 89 rings in the hoard, some with inset carved gems, Others shaped like snakes.

Silver pendant for attaching to a necklace

BITS AND PIECES
Fragments of old necklaces, bracelets, and rings were melted down to make new pieces.

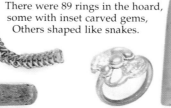

Ingot of silver bullion

This shaped stone found with the hoard is a polishing tool

Transportation, travel, and trade

PERHAPS THE GREATEST GIFT Rome gave the ancient world was the Roman Peace. For the only time in history until then, the entire Mediterranean and the lands around were at peace and under one government. The Roman navy suppressed pirates, and the army laid the famous network of great highways. These roads were built with military needs in mind, but they helped to open up the empire and, with the open seaways, helped to tie the many peoples and provinces together. Trade and prosperity grew. Merchant ships carried the wines of Italy and Spain to Gaul and Britain, while huge freighters, the supertankers of their day, bore the grain harvest of North Africa to feed the people of the city of Rome. Wild animals for the amphitheater were collected from many countries (p. 32). Soldiers, politicians, traders, and even some tourists traveled across the empire, and with them came new fashions and ideas. For instance, the Roman Peace helped Christianity to spread from its Eastern homeland, along the roads and seaways, to the cities of the West.

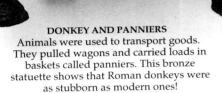

DONKEY AND PANNIERS
Animals were used to transport goods. They pulled wagons and carried loads in baskets called panniers. This bronze statuette shows that Roman donkeys were as stubborn as modern ones!

STORAGE VESSELS
These pottery jars, called *amphorae*, held Italian wine, mostly for selling to other countries. Their shape allowed them to be tightly packed together in the holds of merchant ships. Other shapes of amphora were used to carry olive oil or fish sauce for cooking (p. 44).

Dupondius, worth two asses

As

Aureus, worth 100 asses

Sestertius, worth four asses

Denarius, worth 16 asses

READY MONEY
Coins were minted by the emperor mainly to pay the soldiers and to collect taxes. Almost everyone across the empire used this common money, which made trading simpler. Well-preserved silver *denarii* can be found today as far away as India.

A MERCHANT SHIP
A stone relief from Carthage shows a small ship and its helmsman. In the summer months laden freighters sailed the seas as far as Britain and India. Lacking compasses they hugged the coast, but feared to get too close in case the wind wrecked them on the shore. Sailing was dangerous and usually ceased during the winter.

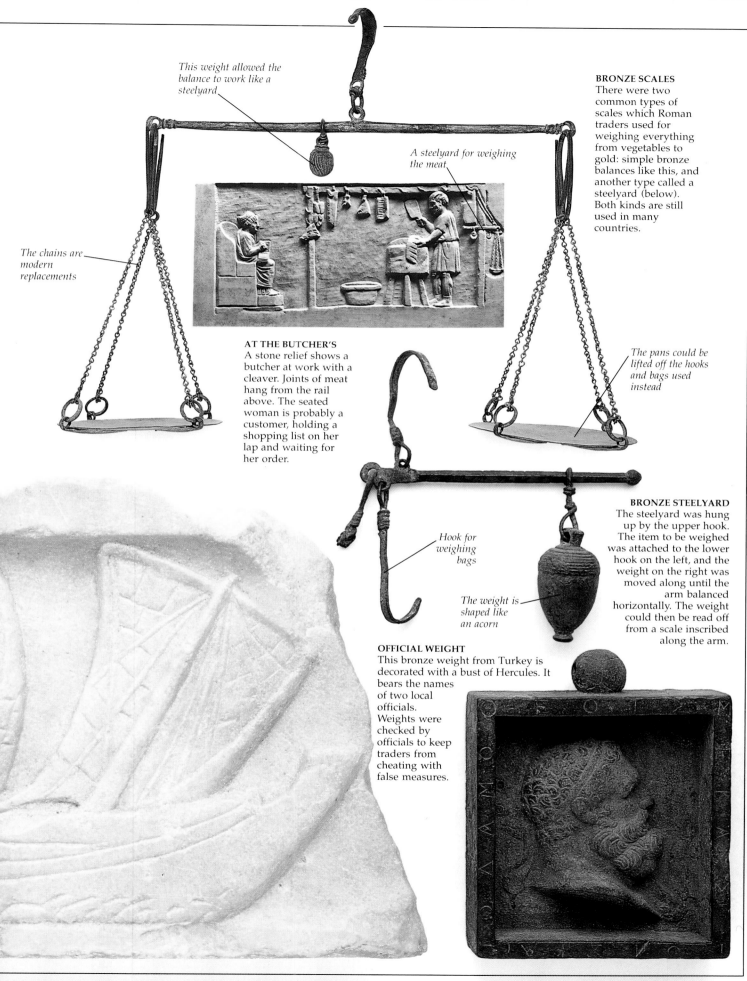

This weight allowed the balance to work like a steelyard

BRONZE SCALES
There were two common types of scales which Roman traders used for weighing everything from vegetables to gold: simple bronze balances like this, and another type called a steelyard (below). Both kinds are still used in many countries.

A steelyard for weighing the meat

The chains are modern replacements

The pans could be lifted off the hooks and bags used instead

AT THE BUTCHER'S
A stone relief shows a butcher at work with a cleaver. Joints of meat hang from the rail above. The seated woman is probably a customer, holding a shopping list on her lap and waiting for her order.

Hook for weighing bags

The weight is shaped like an acorn

BRONZE STEELYARD
The steelyard was hung up by the upper hook. The item to be weighed was attached to the lower hook on the left, and the weight on the right was moved along until the arm balanced horizontally. The weight could then be read off from a scale inscribed along the arm.

OFFICIAL WEIGHT
This bronze weight from Turkey is decorated with a bust of Hercules. It bears the names of two local officials. Weights were checked by officials to keep traders from cheating with false measures.

The twilight of Rome

GREAT CHANGES OVERCAME the Roman Empire after A.D. 200. There were constant clashes with the "barbarians" to the north and the warlike Persians in the east. There was eco-nomic chaos, and frequent civil wars as generals once more struggled for power. Eventually Diocletian and his three co-emperors managed to restore peace, but at a price; the empire groaned under the weight of a growing and corrupt administrative system and an increasingly powerless army. One of Diocletian's successors, Constantine, believed that he came to power with the help of the Christian god, and by his death in A.D. 337 Christianity had not only emerged from the shadows but had become the state religion. By A.D. 400, paganism was declining and being repressed. In A.D. 395 the empire was finally divided into two states, east and west. They were to have very different fates.

A CHRISTIAN FAMILY
This fragment of gold glass depicts a family with the early Christian *chi* (X)-*rho* (P) symbol (made from the first two letters of Christ's name in Greek).

THE LATIN WEST...
Below is a silver statuette representing Rome, the old, pagan, western capital. Both figures come from the 4th-century Esquiline treasure found in Rome.

The 30 pieces of silver paid to Judas for his betrayal

CHRIST ON THE CROSS
A detailed design on an ivory box depicts the crucifixion of Christ and, on the left, Judas hanging himself. It dates from about A.D. 420. Christ was often shown without a beard in Roman times.

Below is a fanciful view of the baptism of Constantine, the first Christian emperor

...AND THE GREEK EAST
Above is a personification of Constantinople, the new eastern capital and Christian city founded by Constantine. Today it is called Istanbul.

The decline of the West

As Christianity triumphed, the western empire was beginning to break up under the strain of military defeat and economic crisis. The Rhine frontier was overrun in A.D. 406, and the German peoples poured into the empire. In A.D. 410 Rome itself was sacked, and in A.D. 476 the last western emperor lost his power. Rome itself had fallen, but the eastern empire lived on.

RADIATE BROOCHES
The Germans were not all the rough warriors the Romans thought them to be. Some were skilled craftsworkers and made spectacular jewelry. The brooches on the left, for example, were made by the Ostrogoths in about A.D. 500 from silver, gold, green glass, and red garnet.

Red garnet inlaid in the gold

Iron spearhead

Two iron arrowheads

WEAPONS OF WAR
These arms, an iron spearhead and two arrowheads, come from the grave of one of the Frankish conquerors of Gaul. By the time these weapons were buried, during the 6th century, the new Frankish kingdom had been established. During these centuries the barbarians were also gradually converted to Christianity.

The barbarians
Rome feared the Germans and other "barbarian" peoples to the north, who were becoming very powerful in the 4th century. When the barbarians finally burst into the western empire they settled in the newly conquered lands and founded many of the states of modern Europe; the Franks turned Gaul into France, and the Angles and Saxons turned Roman Britain into Saxon England.

ATTILA AND THE POPE
The Huns from central Asia were the most feared invaders of all, and they devastated 5th-century Europe. This medieval drawing shows the Pope negotiating with their leader Attila in A.D. 452. It was believed that this saved the city of Rome from further destruction.

The East survives
The heavily populated and wealthy East also experienced wars, but it survived, more and more precariously, until 1453. It still called itself "Roman," but this Greek-speaking Christian state was very different from old Rome, and is today referred to as the Byzantine Empire.

Artemis, the Greek goddess of hunting

MEDALLION
The Christian Byzantines preserved the heritage of their Greek and Roman ancestors in their libraries and treasuries, and their artists still sometimes used pagan images, such as the figure on this sixth-century gold medallion. The classical heritage was rediscovered by the West at the end of the Middle Ages.

BYZANTINE EMPEROR
The bronze steelyard weight (p. 61) on the right depicts a 7th-century emperor. He looks more like a medieval king than a Roman emperor, and the style of art is also very different from earlier times; Byzantium was a medieval state.

Index

Acknowledgments

DK would like to thank:

The Department of Greek and Roman Antiquities, the British Museum for providing ancient artifacts for photography.
Mr. B. Cook and Mr. D. Bailey, The Department of Greek and Roman Antiquities, the British Museum.
Mr. D. Kidd and Mr. D. Buckton, The Department of Medieval and Later Antiquities, the British Museum.
Dr. T. W. Potter and Miss C. Johns, The Department of Prehistoric and Romano-British Antiquities, the British Museum.
Celia Clear, British Museum Publications.
Patsy Vanags of the British Museum Education Service for her assistance with the text.
Emma Cox for her invaluable assistance in making ancient artifacts available for photography.
Alan Meek for the armor and weapons on pp. 82–83.

Andrew Chiakli and Toby Williams for modeling the clothes and armor.
Anita Burger for hairdressing and makeup.
Peter Akkermans, Samantha Bolden, Rupert L. Chapman, Peter Dorrell, Peter Rea, Dianne Rowan, and Kathryn W. Tubb for invaluable further assistance.
Jane Coney for providing props.
Ermine Street Guard, pp. 90–91.

Jacquie Gulliver and Thomas Keenes for their work on the initial stages of the book; Céline Carez, Bernadette Crowley, Claire Gillard, Djinn von Noorden, Louise Pritchard, and Helena Spiteri for editorial assistance; Jane Coney, Earl Neish, Manisha Patel, and Liz Sephton for design assistance; Lester Cheeseman for his desktop publishing expertise.

Model maker: David Donkin

Illustrations: Peter Bull, Eugene Fleury, John Hutchinson, and John Woodcock

Maps: Eugene Fleury and Sallie Alane Reason

Indexer: Marion Dent
Assistant Editor: Anna Scobie
Designer: Maggie Tingle

Picture credits
(l =left r=right t=top b=below c=center a=above)

Aerofilms: 102bc.
Aldus Archive/Syndication International: 101cl.
J.C. Allen: 7b, 19cb, 39tr.
Allsport: Gray Mortimore 81cl;   Vandystadt 81c.
American School of Classical Studies, Athens: 70tlb.
Ancient Art & Architecture Collection: 23tl, 41tl, 52tr, 54cl, 80tl, 85cr, 104bl, 118c.
Ashmolean Museum, Oxford: 24c, 49tl.
Bildarchiv Preussicher Kulturbestitz (Antikenmuseum Berlin): 71tr.
Werner Braun: 6b, 43cr.
Birmingham Museum and Art Galleries: 40b.
Bridgeman Art Library: 34br detail, 43tr detail; /Atkinson Art Gallery, Southport 41b; /Bible Society, London 38cr, 39cl, 40tl, 41cr; /Christies, London 24bl, 41cl; /De Morgan Foundation 53tl; /Fine Art Society 76br; /Guildhall Library 12b, 22c detail;

/House of Masks, Delos 60tl; /Musée des Beaux-Arts, Nantes 41tr; /Musee Crozatier, Le Puy en Velay 92cl; National Gallery, London 54cb; /Prado, Madrid 39bc; /Private Collection 40cr, 68tl; /Royal Library, Stockholm 39cr; /Antiken Museum, Staatliche Museen, W. Berlin 100cr, 104tl, 112cl; /Staatliche Antikensammlungen, Munchen 74c; /Vatican Museums 75b.
British Film Institute: 113br.
Trustees of the British Museum: 8bl, 22cr, 58tr, 58bl, 58br, 59c, 59bc, 59br, 60bl, 74tr, 74br, 92br, 97tl, 97bl, 100tl, 101bl, 107tr, 120bl.
J. Allan Cash Photolibrary: 95cl.
© Dr. John Coates: 83cb.
Photo DAI Athens: 52c (neg. Mykonos 70).
Michael Dixon, Photo Resources: 97br, 98tl, 114tr, 115bl.
Dr. P. Dorrell, Institute of Archaeology: 8cr.
Egyptian Museum, Cairo: 16c.
Ekdotike Athenon: 78bl.
E.T. Archive: 84cr; /Victoria & Albert Museum 7tl.
Mary Evans Picture Library: 17br, 27cr, 28tr, 54tl, 54c, 54bl, 66cl, 69cl, 72tr, 73tl, 74tr, 74br, 75c, 75bc, 76tl, 76c, 76cr, 77, 80b, 82c, 85cb, 87br, 88cl, 94bl, 96cr, 110tl, 124bc, 125tr.
Werner Forman Archive: 109tr.
Giraudon Louvre: 27tl.
Sonia Halliday Photographs: 6tl, 6cl, 23c, 45tc, 48tl, 51tc, 51tr, 52bl, 60tr, 65tl, 65tr, 65c, 71c, 80cr, 112tl.
Hamburger Kunsthalle: 30tl detail.
Robert Harding Picture Library: 10cl, 33br, 36bl, 38cl, 117tl, 123 tr; /G. White 58c, 72c, 77bl, 78bc, 79cl.
Michael Holford: 18–19b, 24, 27cl, 30–31, 46tr, 47tr, 49bl, 58tl, 60br, 61c.
© Hulton Picture Co: 81b.
Image Bank: 77bc, 78tl, 79br.
Dept. of Antiquities, Israel Museum: 15t, 20bl, 23tr, 38cl.
Simon James: 92br, 102tl, 103cl, 103cr, 104tl, 106cr, 115tl, 117tc.
Kobal Collection: 85c, 114cl.
Kunsthistorisches Museum, Vienna: 10–11b.
Louvre/© Reunion des Musees Nationaux: 98–99b.
Mansell Collection: 39tl, 51tl, 52tl, 52tc, 84tl, 87t, 93tl.
The National Gallery, London: 45cl detail, 49cr.
National Maritime Museum, Haifa: 26–27b.
Anne Pearson: 64br.
Photostage/© Donald Cooper 73tc.
Zev Radovan: 6cb, 13cl, 15cr, 43c; /Scala 45tl.
Royal Ontario Museum: 59tl.
Scala: /Citta del Vaticano, Rome 93tr; /Delphi Museum 64bl; /Heraklion Museum 48b; /MNA 76b, 80cl; /Musei Capitolini, Rome 116tl; /Museo Civico, Albenga 122cl; /Museo della Terme, Rome 76cl, 96bl; /Museo Nationale, Athens 51bc, 60cl; /Museo Nazionale, Naples 116br, 119tl; The Vatican Museums 72b.
Jamie Simpson: 12c.
Sotheby's, London: 7tr.
SPADEM: 52br, 61tr, 62tr, 63bl, 85b.
Amoret Tanner: 12tl.
Victoria & Albert Museum: 39bl.
ZEFA: 7c, 34bl; /Damm 65cl; Konrad Helbig 59tc, 66tl; Starfoto 84c.

Every effort has been made to trace the copyright holders of photographs. The publisher apologizes for any unintentional omissions and would be pleased, in such cases, to amend future editions.